The
Islamic Year

Surahs, Stories and
Celebrations

Noorah Al-Gailani • Chris Smith

Illustrated by Helen Williams

With a foreword by
The Rt Hon Baroness Uddin

Hawthorn Press

Published by Hawthorn Press, Hawthorn House,
1 Lansdown Lane, Stroud, Gloucestershire, GL5 1BJ, UK
Tel: (01453) 757040 Fax: (01453) 751138
email: info@hawthornpress.com
Website: **www.hawthornpress.com**

Drawings and cover illustration © Helen Williams
Cover design and typesetting by Hawthorn Press, Stroud, Glos.
Printed by The Bath Press, Bath
Reprinted 2004

Printed on environmentally friendly chlorine-free paper manufactured from renewable forest stock

British Library Cataloguing in Publication Data applied for

ISBN 1 903458 14 5

Dedication

To Khalah Khulood,
for her loving care,
and the Zakariyya Tray she made.

To Peter and Dione
for their generosity and loving care.

A sound and very helpful resource for teachers – it recognises the internal pluralism of both religious ideas and cultural expressions which characterises the Muslim communities in this country and globally.

Professor Jorgen Nielsen, Department of Theology,
University of Birmingham

The stories are ripe for re-telling – I enjoyed their warmth and humour. They make the life and teaching of the Prophet Muhammad caring and accessible.

Chris East, Advisory Teacher, Waltham Forest

Contents

Contents

Acknowledgements

We would like to thank the interviewees, who kindly shared with us their personal memories of Muslim festivals and their celebrations: Mrs. Samira Al-Jebechi; the late Mrs. Muna Tawfiq; Mrs. Jalila Al-Gailani and Mr. Moufak Dib; Mrs. Nawal Al-Tel; Mrs. Mahitab Muhammad Haider; Mrs. Khalida Khan, Mrs. Humera Khan, and Mrs. Meher Basit; Mrs. Selma El-Rayah and Mr. Osman Elnusairi; Miss Hussa Khumairi, Ms. Samia Shibli, Mr. Ludfi Rahman, Mr. Hassan Al-Qeek , Mr. Shafiq Qurajali and Kenan.

Thanks also to Mr. Khalid Nabris, Mr. Michael Marran, Dr. Lamia Al-Gailani Werr, Mrs. Janice Al-Gailani, and Miss Wijdan Maher for their encouragement, help and support. Thanks also to the staff of the Resource Centre at The Commonwealth Institute, London, for their help in providing information and access to their library.

Thanks also to Mr. Usamah K. Ward of The Muslim Educational Trust, for his valuable and careful comments and to Professor Jorgen Nielsen, Chris East and Judith Large for their excellent suggestions.

Foreword

I am heartened by the publication of this book which, in promoting positive understanding of Islam – a major and growing world religion – can help inspire knowledge and build bridges.

Today we live in a world of increasing conflict where, I believe, each one of us can choose to nourish the goodness among us; or not – with inevitable and dangerous consequences. Many of the conflicts involve countries with a predominantly Muslim population – Iraq, Palestine, Kashmir and of course Afghanistan. Often these conflicts are portrayed as being between 'Western' and Islamic' values, an unhelpful and dangerous simplification, particularly since the catastrophic incident of September 11th. So this book will arrive in an era where there is urgent need for clarity – accurate explanation about Islam as it lives amongst ordinary people going about their daily lives.

In a recent exhibition at the British Museum, a group of girls from a Muslim club in Exeter were asked to make a banner expressing their feeling about being a Muslim in Britain. One of the slogans on the banner read, simply:

'Remember that we are human too.'

This plea from young British-born citizens illustrates how much isolation and prejudice some Muslims living in the West feel in the current volatile political climate. Recent discussion on the issue of citizenship has become confused in the face of a new world refugee crisis. In reality Muslims have been citizens of Britain for over two centuries, and form an enormously diverse group, coming from countries throughout the globe. There is a corresponding range of opinions and attitudes to the Muslim faith, with individuals interpreting the teaching in different ways to suit their own cultural context.

We therefore need to ensure that information is made available in a factual way which builds on understanding, embraces this huge diversity, and at all costs avoids further stereotyping. We need to reinstate the knowledge of what Islam and Muslims have in common with Christianity, Judaism and other faiths.

We need also to educate the world about the contribution of Islam and connect it to the everyday context of people's lives. For instance, it can be the pride of every Muslim that Islam has shared in a prominent way in developing the arts, heritage, and architecture throughout Europe. Islam contributed to the foundation of western civilisation through the introduction of paper, mathematics (algebra), trigonometry, modern medicine (particularly ophthalmology) and coffee – to name but a few. It is known that the rituals of Cambridge and Oxford still owe their origin directly to the Al-Azhar University of Egypt.

For those working as educators, seeking to interpret Islam to non-Muslim audiences, this book offers a *pot pourri* of excellent tools. While there have been many excellent books in English summarising Islam for Muslims, less is available for the purpose of multi-cultural education, at a time when such education is critical to social cohesion and strengthening understanding.

This book offers a number of approaches to assist educators facing the challenge of dealing with:
- how to respectfully communicate the spirit of one faith to those with a different religious belief;

- how to engage and enter into dialogue with those without religious belief of any kind;
- how to confront stereotypes and gain insight into the variety and diversity of Muslim countries, each with their own cultural heritage.

I like the way this book is structured around the life of the Prophet Muhammad, providing a coherent narrative to explain the way Muslims celebrate their faith. The story is told in a simple and engaging manner, while keeping the sacred spirit of the original texts. In this way the five pillars of Islam and the various festivals can be understood in relation to the Prophet's life and teaching, the heart of the Islamic narrative.

The Prophet's teaching includes promotion of values that are common to most spiritual traditions. These are explored through a number of folktales from different countries of the Muslim world. These are not Islamic stories as such, and some may even predate Islam, yet they provide an accessible account to illustrate these values, especially with younger people in mind. It is one thing to tell a class that it is good to be generous, yet quite another to tell the story of Abu Kassim's boots, a comedy invariably popular with children and adults alike, and generate discussion to ask what can be learned from it. This is a good method for effective teaching, making learning more fun.

The craft activities in the book will provide another excellent vehicle for engaging students with issues related to Islam.

Finally, the festivals themselves are explained in a simple and clear way, relating them to each aspect of the Prophet's life and teaching that they celebrate. The descriptions emphasise both unity and diversity. There is information on some differences between celebrations in different countries of the Muslim world, and reference to the question of why some women wear the scarf, while others choose not to. The images of women in this book reflect the diversity throughout the Muslim world.

There is a story that a new cathedral was once being built in a certain town. The architect visiting the building site noticed three men building a wall. Two looked sad and the third happy:

He asked the first what he was doing:
'Laying bricks,' came the answer with a scowl.
He asked the second sad man the same question:
'I have to work here to earn money for my family.'
The third, happy man said:
'I'm building a great cathedral, a place where people may find peace, and be closer to God.'

No one book can answer all our soul-searching questions and counter centuries of prejudice, but every attempt at inspiring new understanding must be saluted in earnest. I trust this book will provide a meaningful way to inspire educators and their students, and lead a new generation to freedom from the shackles of prejudice and mistrust.

My appreciation to Noorah Al-Gailani and Dr Chris Smith for their courage, hard work and dedication in bringing out this detailed guide to Islam, with future generations of children in mind.

Baroness Uddin
House of Lords
Houses of Parliament
London
June 2002

Preface

This book is the fruit of collaboration between a Muslim educator and a storyteller.

Noorah Al-Gailani MA is a Muslim of Iraqi origin, who has taught Islam to Muslim children in various settings. Noorah teaches through games, creative activities and stories, and believes – as an educator – that it is important for children to learn to think for themselves about their faith, to develop their own understanding of Muslim teaching. Noorah currently works as the curator of Islamic Civilisations for Glasgow Museum Service.

Chris Smith PhD is a British storyteller and musician who lived for many years in the Middle East where he developed knowledge of Arab and Muslim culture. Chris works regularly with the British Museum Education department. His work in schools aims to promote knowledge and understanding about Arab and Islamic culture.

Negative stereotyping of Muslims has been endemic in Western culture for many years. To counter negative influences, therefore, it is so important to offer children positive experience of Islam, especially for children who have no direct experience of Islam or Muslims. Story and craft provide excellent vehicles for such experiences, building on familiar activities that children enjoy, while at the same time raising important issues for teachers to work with.

I (Chris) remember teaching a class on Islam to a group of nine-year-olds in an inner city school. I started by asking if anyone in the class was a Muslim. The response was sniggering and then laughter. When I asked why it was clear that, for them, Muslims were a rather distant and somehow threatening idea. Of course there are no Muslims in our class!

By the end of the storytelling session the group was excited and inquisitive. There was a barrage of questions and not enough time to answer them. The children in the group practising another faith were struck by similarities between Islam and their own religious practices. For others the stories were fun, intriguing and thought-provoking. Some started making connections: 'That picture is like the one the taxi drivers have in their cars. Does that mean they are Muslims?'

In this way Muslims and their faith became a little more understood; less alien, less threatening, more familiar, more interesting. Our wish for this book is that it may contribute to such understanding.

Chris Smith, Oxford
Noorah Al-Gailani, London

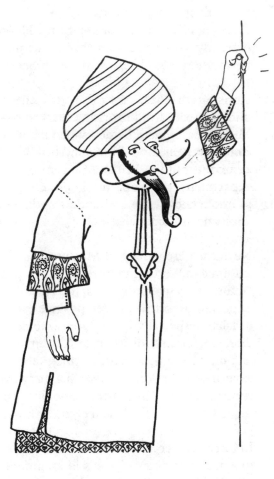

Introduction

Fourteen centuries have passed since the Prophet Muhammad lived and taught in the desert towns of Makkah and Madinah. Within a century of his death his followers ruled an empire stretching from Spain in the West through North Africa to the borders of China in the East. Today, it is estimated, there are more than a billion Muslims world-wide who follow the Prophet's teachings.

Lack of awareness in the West means that Islam is frequently connected with conflict in the news. Radical, political Islam continues to make the headlines, encouraging a negative stereotype of Islam as violent, anti-democratic and supportive of terrorism. There is an urgent need to counter this trend with information and understanding. We hope this publication can contribute to this goal.

We intend the book to be used as a tool for multicultural education, offering information and ideas for ways to explain Islam and its festivals to non-Muslims in schools and other community settings. Our hope is that it will enable educators to present aspects of Islam in an interesting and accurate way to students.

The book is organised around the story of the life of the Prophet Muhammad. This framework was chosen because each of the main Muslim festivals refers to a particular event in the Prophet's life. We felt that the significance of each individual festival could best be understood in relation to this overall narrative.

The festivals we have chosen are those days of particular religious significance in the Muslim calendar. They may or may not be actively celebrated in a particular country, but their religious significance is acknowledged by all Muslims. They are:

- The Prophet's Birthday (Milad-an-Nabi);
- The Night of Destiny (Laylat-ul-Qadr);
- The Night Journey and Ascension (Al-Isra' wa Al-Miraj.)
- New Year (Hijrah);
- The Feast at the End of Ramadan (Id-ul-Fitr);
- The Feast of Sacrifice (Id-ul-Adha).

The material in this book has been organised as follows:

- Each chapter begins with a quote from the Qur'an and a story from the life of the Prophet. These sections, if read one after another, provide an account of main events in the Prophet's life, from his birth to death. In this way the book can be used as a general primer on Islam as well as to focus specifically on festivals.
- Each chapter then discusses the religious significance of the particular festival, and ways that it is celebrated in various countries.
- Next we offer a few suggestions on activities for the classroom or home, to deepen understanding of the festival, and to engage with it actively.
- Finally, traditional folktales are presented from various Islamic countries (i.e. where Muslims are a majority). These stories illustrate a particular theme that may be associated with the festival and its teachings.

This overall scheme is shown in the table overleaf.

Organisation of material in the book

Chapter title	Main story	Corresponding festival	Theme for folktales
1. Before Muhammad	Abraham and Ishmael build the Sacred House (the Ka'bah) at Makkah.		
2. Birth	Muhammad is born in Makkah.	Prophet's Birth	Obedience to the will of God
3. Prophethood Begins	Muhammad receives the first revelation of the Qur'an in Makkah.	The Night of Destiny	Faith
4. A Miraculous Journey	Muhammad makes a miraculous journey to heaven where he meets past Prophets and receives profound teachings.	The Night Journey and Ascension	Prayer
5. A New Beginning	After persecution Muhammad flees Makkah and settles in the town of Madinah.	The New Year	Travel and danger
6. Establishing Community	Muhammad establishes a Muslim community in Madinah, and reveals many teachings concerning community life.	Ramadan and the Fast-Breaking Feast	Generosity
7. Homecoming	Muhammad returns to Makkah, which he conquers without bloodshed. Four years later he dies.	Pilgrimage and the Feast of Sacrifice	Equality and justice

The scheme can also provide a context for explaining the five core teachings of Islam, according to the time in the prophet's life when they were revealed.

The Five Pillars of Islam

Pillar	Time of revelation
1. Declaration of Faith (Shehadah)	Night of Destiny (Ch. 3)
2. Prayer (Salah)	Night Journey and Ascension (Ch. 4)
3. Fasting (Sawm)	Life in Madinah (Ch.6)
4. Giving to the Poor (Zakah)	Life in Madinah (Ch. 6)
5. Pilgrimage (Hajj)	Return to Makkah (Ch. 7)

Our presentation of the life of Muhammad is based on established Islamic sources. The discussions of festivals and ways of celebration are taken from interviews with Muslims from relevant countries, aiming to reflect the core teaching common to all Muslims as well as the diversity of ways of celebration.

We envisage the book as a reference text for teachers and educators, and have tried to write the various sections so that each can be read independently. This has led to a small amount of necessary repetition.

It is common for Muslims to add a formal blessing whenever the Prophet's name is mentioned. However, as this book has been written for use by non-Muslims we have decided not to include such a blessing, assuming that those who wish to do so will add the blessing themselves when reading from the book.

It is important for educators to understand the differences between Sunni and Shi'ah Muslims, and to this end we have dedicated a small annex to the development of Islam after the life of the Prophet, including details of the origin of the Sunni/Shi'ah division and the celebration of the Ashura festival of the Shi'ah. Our choice to omit this festival from the main chapters was simply because it does not fit within the narrative of the life of the Prophet himself. It is not intended to reflect any judgement on the importance of this date in the Islamic calendar.

We have chosen to visually illustrate this book with many images, both for the main narratives, and for the stories and activities. Careful consideration has been given to depicting images of people, within the Islamic tradition. We believe that, as this book's aim is to raise awareness and appreciation of Islam and its cultures amongst non-Muslims, especially children, the educational value of these illustrations is crucial.

In addition, deciding on illustrations of religious stories provided a particular dilemma. For many Muslims it would be considered inappropriate to include actual representations of the Prophet's face, while others might feel any representation of prophets or angels to be out of place.

On the other hand there are traditions in Islam for which such representations are used, for example in Abbasid, Ottoman and Persian Islamic art. While wishing to respect the views of those who consider visual representations of prophets or angels inappropriate, one of the main themes of the book is to promote the idea of diversity. We have sought to honour both these principles by avoiding any direct representation of the Prophet's face, while including one or two images of other prophets and angelic figures.

Concerning illustration of the folktales and descriptions of the festivals themselves, we have again tried to reflect diversity in the various styles of clothing and dress in various countries, including the different ways in which Muslim women dress.

Each chapter includes a number of verses from the Qur'an. Translations are never as good as the original text, but we have taken care to use translations which reflect, as closely as possible, the exact meaning intended in the Arabic original.

Finally, regarding transliteration, our main aim has been simplicity rather than academic rigour. We want to make it as easy as possible for people with no knowledge of Arabic to read the text with a 'good enough' pronunciation. To this end we have adopted the spelling recommended by the British Curriculum Authority for use by teachers (see glossary for guide to pronunciation). We have chosen to use the Biblical names for the prophets rather than their Arabic equivalents, to make the stories more accessible to non-Muslim readers.

Chapter 1

BEFORE MUHAMMAD

Abraham said to his Lord:
'O our Lord, I have made some of my offspring dwell in a valley without cultivation, by Your Sacred House, in order that they may establish regular prayer. So fill the hearts of some among men with love towards them, and feed them with fruits, so that they may give thanks. O our Lord! Truly you do know what we conceal and what we reveal, for nothing whatever is hidden from God, whether on earth or in heaven.'

The Qur'an: *Surat Ibrahim*

Abraham and the House of God

For Muslims, the holiest place on earth is the city of Makkah (often spelled 'Mecca') in the Arabian Desert. As well as being the birthplace of the Prophet Muhammad, it is the site of a holy shrine known as the Ka'bah, also known as *the House of God*. Every year millions of Muslims make a pilgrimage to Makkah to visit the House of God.

The Middle East in the Sixth Century A.D.

The story of Makkah begins with the Prophet Abraham. This is the same prophet, recognised by both Christians and Jews, who appears in the Old Testament of the Bible. (Abraham is known as Ibrahim to Arabs and Muslims.)

Abraham and the fire

Long ago a prophet named Abraham was born in the town of Ur in Mesopotamia (modern day Iraq). At that time the people of Babel worshipped stone statues and wooden carvings as if they were gods. Abraham's father worked as a craftsman, making carvings and statues. Abraham believed in the worship of a single, universal God, and called on his townspeople to do the same, but they ignored him. On one occasion he went into their temple and destroyed their carvings and statues, and they decided he should be punished with death by burning. They tied his hands and feet with ropes, built a huge bonfire with Abraham on top, and set it alight. But as the flames blazed around Abraham, the onlookers noticed that he was smiling. The flames did not hurt him, and only burned through the ropes that held him.

Abraham takes Ishmael to the desert

After this miracle Abraham travelled to many lands, finally settling with his wife, Sarah, in Palestine. As the years went by Sarah did not give birth to any children. They wanted children so badly that Sarah suggested that Abraham take a second wife. Abraham agreed and married his Egyptian maid, Hajar, who soon gave birth to a baby boy, Ishmael. Once Ishmael was born Sarah became more and more jealous. Soon she couldn't bear to see the baby and his mother, and asked Abraham to take them away to a distant place so she would never have to see them again.

Abraham was a holy man who tried to see the will of God in all things. When Sarah made her request Abraham felt that it was God's will that Ishmael be taken away, and so he agreed. Abraham, Hajar and baby Ishmael set out, by camel, on a long journey until they came to a stretch of barren desert, without people, water or food. Abraham sensed that this was the right place to camp. The next day he left his wife and child there with a single water skin and a sack of dates, and returned to Sarah in Palestine.

As Abraham left, Hajar called out to him again and again, 'Abraham! Where are you going? Why do you leave us in the empty valley without people or any other thing!'

Abraham heard her cries but said nothing, continuing to walk away. Finally she called out, 'Did God order you to do this?'

Abraham turned and smiled at her. 'Yes, it was God,' he said.

'Then he will not desert us,' she replied, and returned to her baby as Abraham walked away.

Ishmael finds water

After a few days their supplies of water and food had run out. Hajar was so hungry and thirsty she could no longer produce milk for her son to drink. Ishmael cried and cried until, unable to bear his suffering, Hajar left him lying in the sand and walked away so that she would not have to watch him die.

She climbed a hill and looked out over the next valley hoping to see someone who might help, but saw no one; nothing but desert sand. She climbed down the hill and up another close by looking for help, but again there was no one in sight. In panic she ran between these hills seven times, hoping to catch sight of someone who could help. After she had completed the seventh climb she heard a voice asking her if she was looking for rain. Hajar looked down into the valley and saw an angel standing next to Ishmael. As she watched he pressed his heel into the sand. Moments later, water began to gush from the place where the angel had been.

Praising God, Hajar rushed to the spring and filled her water skin, then returned to her baby to feed him. The angel told her not to fear, saying that one day Ishmael and Abraham would build God's house in this place.

The spring, which runs to this day, is known as the spring of Zamzam, 'the well of abundant waters'. Soon travellers came to the spring for water, and asked Hajar if they might settle there. She agreed, and in time the town of Makkah grew up around the spring.

Abraham and Ishmael build the House of God

Many years later Abraham was travelling to Syria, when an angel appeared in front of him, holding the reins of a winged spirit horse, *the Buraq*. With Abraham riding the horse they flew together high above the earth. Looking down over many lands, the angel asked Abraham to pick a spot where the first Sacred House should be built. Abraham pointed to a place, in the middle of a desert, where a small settlement could be seen around a spring. Unknown to him, Abraham had chosen the place where he had once left Hajar and Ishmael, now the thriving settlement of Makkah.

Following the angel's instructions, Abraham returned to Makkah, to be reunited with this wife and son. Together Abraham and Ishmael built the Sacred House, and re-established there the worship of the one God. This tradition was continued after Abraham's death by Ishmael and his descendants for many generations.

The Prophets of Islam

What is a prophet?

A prophet is a spokesman for God, someone who was inspired to speak God's message and tell his purpose and judgement to other people.

Muslims believe in all the prophets of the Bible, Old and New Testaments. They also believe that God in some cases sends holy books with his prophets. Muhammad is considered the last of these prophets. He is considered a direct messenger of God, with the duty of revealing the Qur'an, Islam's holy book.

In the Qur'an, God says that he has sent a messenger to every nation on earth; and that there is no nation without a prophet. Muslims believe that Muhammad was simply reviving that ancient belief in the one true God as taught by various prophets before him. Christianity and Judaism are respected as pointing to the same truth of one God.

For example, in Palestine there is a shrine to Moses (Nabi Musa, in Arabic). Every year, at Easter time, there is a traditional festival in which Muslims travel to the shrine from all over the country and camp out for up to a week in the open before returning home.

It says in the Qur'an that God has chosen to mention some of the prophets in the Qur'an, but that there are many others which He has chosen not to mention. This means, that in addition to all the prophets mentioned in the Bible and the Qur'an, there have been many others.

What do prophets do?

The prophet's main duty is to call people to lead a good life: that is, to fulfil their duty and lead an honest and honourable life, worshipping God, doing good and avoiding evil.

Which prophets are mentioned in the Qur'an (and also in the Bible)?

Prophets mentioned in the Qur'an	Biblical equivalent
Adam	Adam
Idris	Enoch
Nuh	Noah
Hud	
Salih	
Ibrahim	Abraham
Ismael	Ishmael
Ishaq	Issac
Lut	Lot
Ya'qub	Jacob
Yusef	Joseph
Shuaib	
Musa	Moses
Harun	Aaron
Dawud	David
Suleiman	Solomon
Ilias	Elijah
Al-Yasa	Elisha
Dhul-Kifl	Ilyas
Ayub	Job
Yunus	Jonah
Zakariyya	Zachariah
Yahya	John
'Isa	Jesus
Muhammad	

Zakariyya said: O my Lord how shall I have a son, when my wife is barren and I have grown quite decrepit from old age? The Lord said: So Your Lord has said, that is easy for Me: I did indeed create you before, when you had been nothing! Zakariyya said: O my Lord, give me a sign. He said: Your sign shall be that you shall not speak to people for three nights, though you are not dumb. So Zakariyya came out to his people from his chamber and indicated to them to celebrate God's praises in the morning and in the evening.

From the Qur'an: *Surat Maryam*

The Festival of the Prophet Zakariyya

In various Muslims countries there is a tradition of festivals celebrating the life of a particular prophet. The following example comes from Iraq, where the Prophet Zakariyya is honoured every year. This is his story as told in the Qur'an.

Long ago there lived a prophet called Zakariyya, who spent his life teaching about God. As he grew older he realised that soon he would die. Zakariyya wondered who would carry on his work when he died. Zakariyya was married but he had no children to carry on his work.

Zakariyya prayed, asking God to find the right person to carry on his work after he died:

'Lord, my bones are weak, and my hair shines silver with age. My prayers have always been answered by you. Please, send me a son who will be my heir. May he be noble and worthy!'

God replied: 'Rejoice, Zakariyya! You shall be given a son, and he shall be called John (Yahya in Arabic): the first man to be given this name.'

Zakariyya was amazed at God's words:

'How shall I have a son, Lord, when my wife is barren, and I am an old man? Give me a sign to show that this will occur!' he asked.

God replied:

'For three days and three nights you shall be bereft of speech, though otherwise sound in body. This will be the sign that what I say is true.'

At this Zakariyya came out of the temple unable to speak, and using sign language he instructed his people to celebrate God in both the morning and in the evening.

Later, John was born. As he grew up God blessed him at a tender age with the gifts of wisdom and good judgement. He was blessed with love for all creatures, and was a joy to his parents. John was later to prepare the way for Jesus, who was coming to renew and re-interpret God's revelation.

Celebrating Zakariyya in Iraq

The feast of Zakariyya is held on the first Sunday in the Muslim month of Sha'ban (see Chapter 5 for details of the Muslim calendar).

If a couple is without children, there is a tradition of praying for a child on this day, just as Zakariyya did. If a child is then conceived, it is traditional to commemorate this by preparing a 'Zakariyya Tray' every year.

This tradition involves fasting the whole day, breaking fast at sunset, and setting up a 'Zakariyya Tray' to celebrate the child's birth.

Zakariyya's Tray

This tray is prepared in advance, and holds specific items including: candles, green vegetation (orange tree leaves, and other green bush stems and leaves), plain white yoghurt, wheat bread, water from a well, and water vessels (with a spout for the boys in the family, and with a round neck for the girls in the family). The tray also contains boiled sweets, raisins, sesame seeds, fruits, nuts, and date syrup.

Breaking the fast

At sunset, with the call for prayer, the candles on the tray are lit. The 'break-fast' meal will take place soon after, and the main dish must be *Dolma be-al-Silig* (stuffed Swiss chard); and the sweet dish would be *Zerdah wa Halib,* a traditional Iraqi rice pudding.

If the lunar month of Sha'ban falls outside the Swiss chard season, people will plant the chard seeds two weeks before the due Sunday, to ensure that they have this type of chard for the meal, even if the leaves are only small.

Lighting the candles and making a wish

Relatives and neighbours are welcomed to share the meal and light a candle or make a wish. It is customary for a woman seeking to bear a child to wish for one by a 'Zakariyya Tray' of a neighbour or relative. She will insert a pin into a candle when making her wish to God, promising to set up a tray from the following year onwards, if she is blessed with a child.

Activity Ideas

- ✦ Making a model of the Ka'bah
- ✦ Making a mobile to celebrate the prophets
- ✦ Making a Zakariyya Tray
- ✦ Cooking Zerdah wa Halib (Iraqi rice pudding)
- ✦ Making a small water vessel for the Zakariyya Tray

Activity 1: making a model of the Ka'bah

The Ka'bah (meaning cube) is a cube-shaped building with a flat roof. It is one room with two columns in the centre holding up its roof. Inside there is also a set of stairs leading to the roof. The house is built of mud brick and tree trunks, and contains one stone, the Black Stone, a meteorite. The stone is considered special as it has come from beyond the earth, and is built into one corner of the Ka'bah.

Since Abraham first built the Ka'bah, this cube structure has been rebuilt many times. The only original part of it is the black stone, a meteorite collected by Ishmael to help his father stand on it while building the Ka'bah, and then later used in the building itself. Since time immemorial, the people of Arabia have covered the Ka'bah with textiles to decorate and protect it from the elements.

After the birth of Islam, it became customary to cover the Ka'bah with a thick, black cloth embroidered with gold thread and decorated with Arabic calligraphy, usually of verses from the Qur'an. Because the sun is so powerful in the desert climate, this cover needs to be changed every year. Until the second half of the 20th Century, the covers were traditionally woven and embroidered in Egypt, and sent as a gift from the people of Egypt to the people of Makkah. Since then, special workshops have been set up in Saudi Arabia to make these covers.

Materials:
White card (minimum thickness 200g)
Scissors and cutter (stencil knife)
Glue
Colouring pens or pencils, or poster colours
Thick felt-tip black pen

The Ka'bah at Makkah

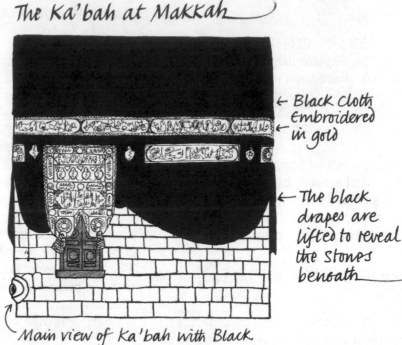

← Black Cloth Embroidered in gold

← The black drapes are lifted to reveal the stones beneath

Main view of Ka'bah with Black Stone framed in a wide, rounded, silver sheet making it project from the corner of the building

Black textile (if not, the effect of the drapes needs to be drawn on the card used to create the Ka'bah)

Or:

white textile, which can be coloured in black using a textile colour or thick, black felt-tip pen

String, or shoelace

Gold or yellow ribbon

Method:

1 Cut out shape of Ka'bah as shown.
2 Draw the door of the Ka'bah and colour it in.
3 Draw the black stone in the right corner and colour.
4 Draw the brick texture and colour.
5 Cut open the door.
6 Glue the box to make the shape of the Ka'bah.
7 Cut out the round base to make the courtyard.
8 Draw and colour the floor tiles.
9 Fix the Ka'bah onto the centre of the base.
10 Prepare the textile cover:
   a. Cut the black textile to shape
   b. Colour the white ribbon
   c. Fix ribbon on to black textile at the right position using glue
   d. Glue the sides of the textile together
   e. Fold top edge and thread in string or shoe lace
   f. Have the two ends of the string or shoe lace visible for tightening when dressing the Ka'bah
11 Dress the Ka'bah model with the textile cover.
12 Tighten the cover from the top.
13 Lift parts of the cover to reveal the door of the Ka'bah and the black stone.

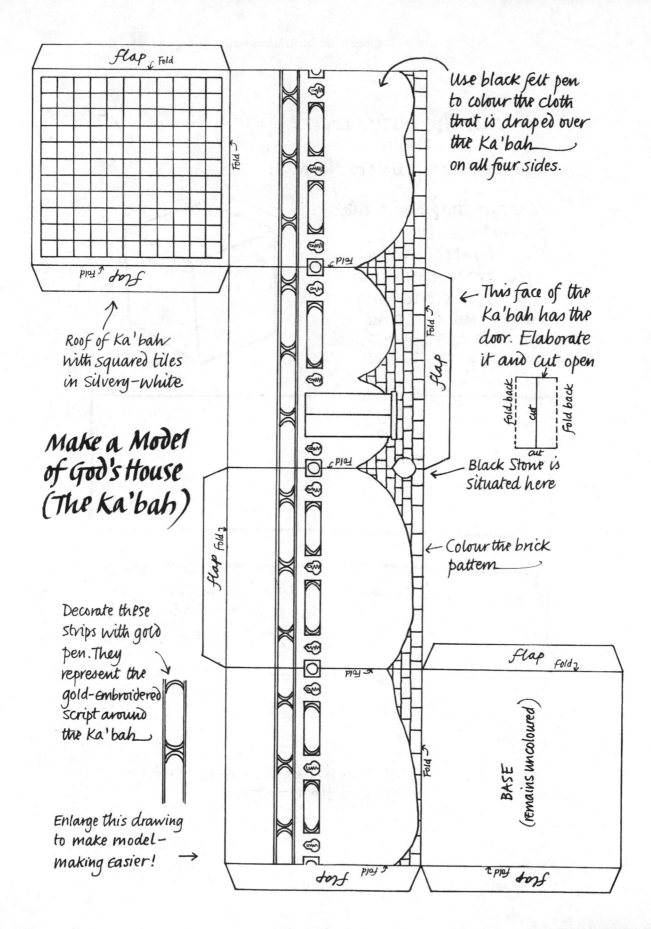

flap Fold

Fold

Use black felt pen to colour the cloth that is draped over the Ka'bah on all four sides.

Roof of Ka'bah with squared tiles in Silvery-white

This face of the Ka'bah has the door. Elaborate it and Cut open

fold back   cut   fold back
cut

Make a Model of God's House (The Ka'bah)

Black Stone is situated here

Colour the brick pattern

Decorate these strips with gold pen. They represent the gold-embroidered script around the Ka'bah

flap Fold

Fold

flap Fold

Fold

Enlarge this drawing to make model-making easier!

Fold

BASE (remains uncoloured)

flap Fold

flap Fold

Prepare the textile cover :

Cut the black textile to shape :

Measure the height and
perimeter of your
Ka'bah model. Add on
a few extra centimetres
(inches) for overlapping
the top and gathering
the cloth to ease round the
corners of the model.

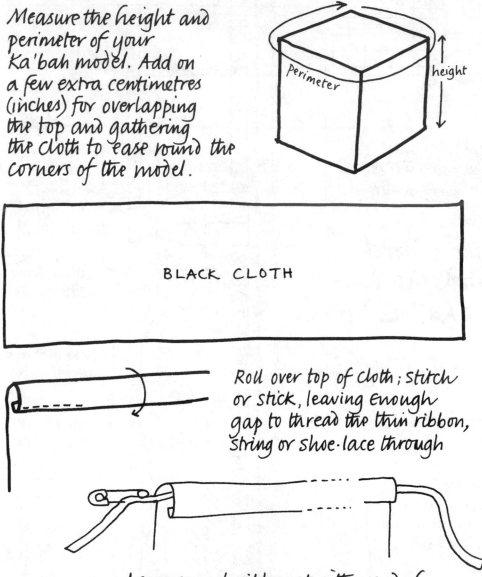

BLACK CLOTH

Roll over top of cloth ; stitch
or stick, leaving enough
gap to thread the thin ribbon,
string or shoe·lace through

Leave enough ribbon at either end of
the cloth, to tie together.

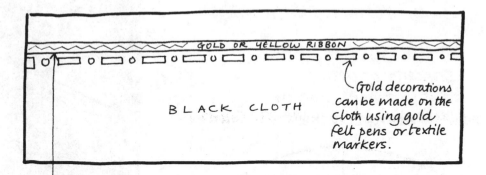

Sew or stick yellow or gold ribbon to represent the gold embroidery on the Ka'bah cloth

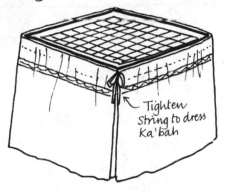

Dress the Ka'bah model with the textile cover. The edges can be oversewn or stuck together, then lift parts of the cover to reveal the door and the black stone

Detail of the Embroidered Curtain
that hangs over door to Ka'bah

Cut out the round base to make the courtyard

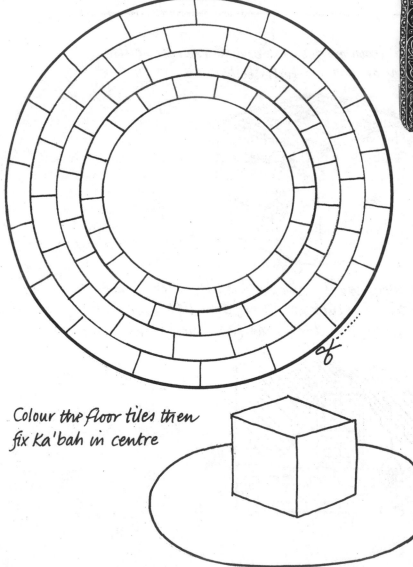

Colour the floor tiles then
fix Ka'bah in centre

12

Activity 2: making a mobile to celebrate the prophets

Total height of mobile approximately 112cm (44 inches). Make sure that you have sufficient height to hang it before you start. If this is too high, reduce the length of the string or fishing line sections of the mobile. Make sure you divide the lengths equally to keep the balance of the mobile.

Materials:

White card for main structure (200g per sheet)
White card for roundels (160g per sheet minimum, or as above)
Scissors and cutter (stencil knife)
String, or fishing line
Hole-puncher
Colouring pens or pencils, or poster colours
Glitter
Pritt Stick, or transparent glue suitable for fixing glitter

Method:

1 Photocopy roundels from the book onto white paper.
2 Photocopy supports, cut them out, stick them on card.
3 Cut and colour supports.
4 Cut out 24 roundels from the white card.
5 Cut out photocopied designed roundels and glue on to the card roundels.
6 Make sure you have the matching prophet name in Arabic and English, one on each side of the roundel.
7 Colour both sides of each roundel.
8 Use glitter to decorate the roundels. Fix glitter with Pritt Stick or glue.
9 Make holes in all the roundels and the supports.
10 Cut out 27 equal lengths of fishing line or string (approximately 12cm, or 5 inches) allowing length for knotting the ends to the roundels and supports.
11 Lay out the mobile on the floor or a large table. Position the supports and roundels in the right order.
12 Start tying them up together. We recommend you start linking each line of roundels together first. Then link the main roundel and the supports together. Lastly, join the lines of roundels with the supports.
13 If the mobile is slightly out of balance, you can stick small pieces of card to the raised side of the supports to weigh them down. Remember to colour these extra pieces of card to camouflage them.
14 Hang the mobile from the ceiling using a staple, small nail or pin.

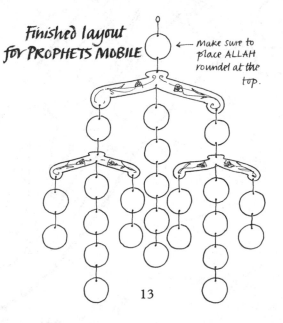

Finished layout for PROPHETS MOBILE

← Make sure to place ALLAH roundel at the top.

14

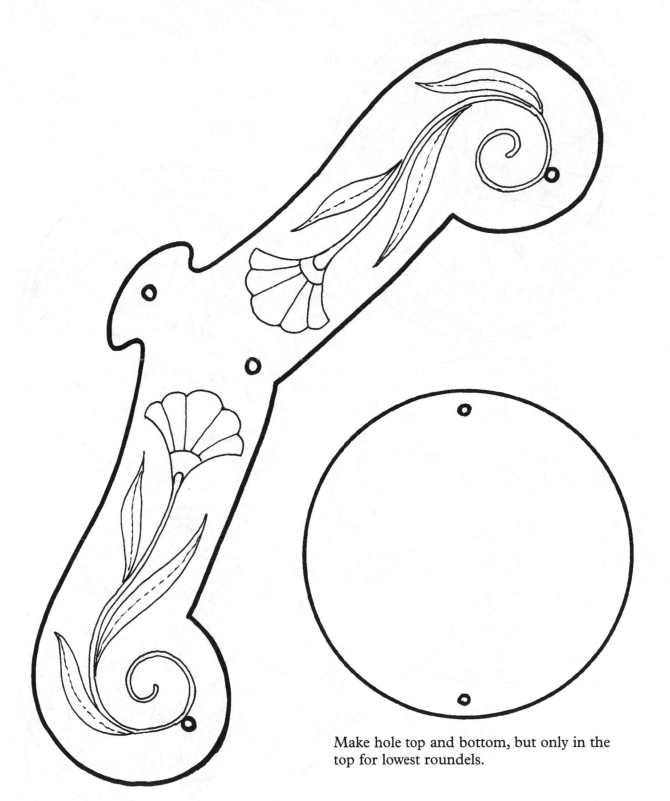

Make hole top and bottom, but only in the
top for lowest roundels.

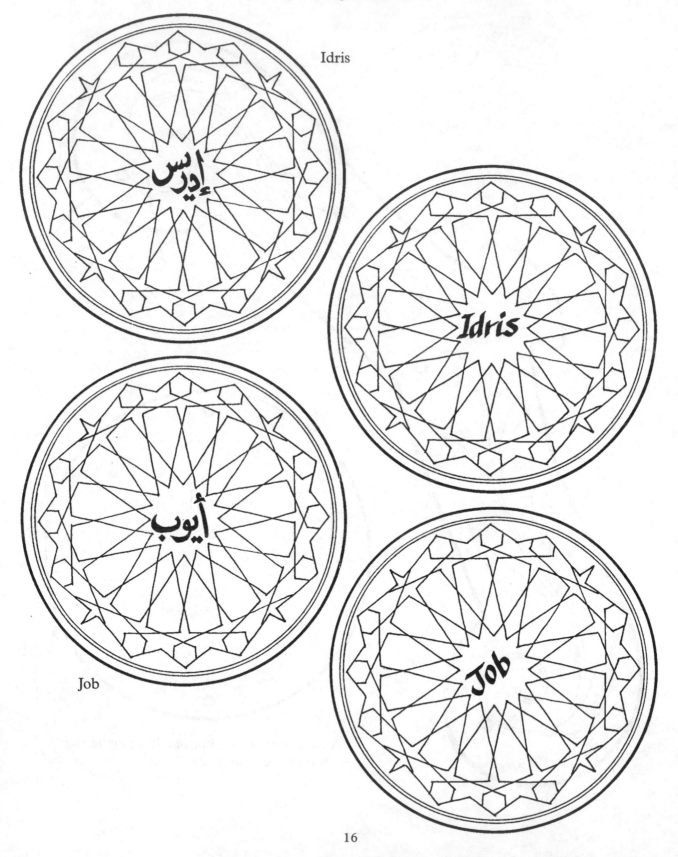

Idris

إدريس

Idris

أيوب

Job

Job

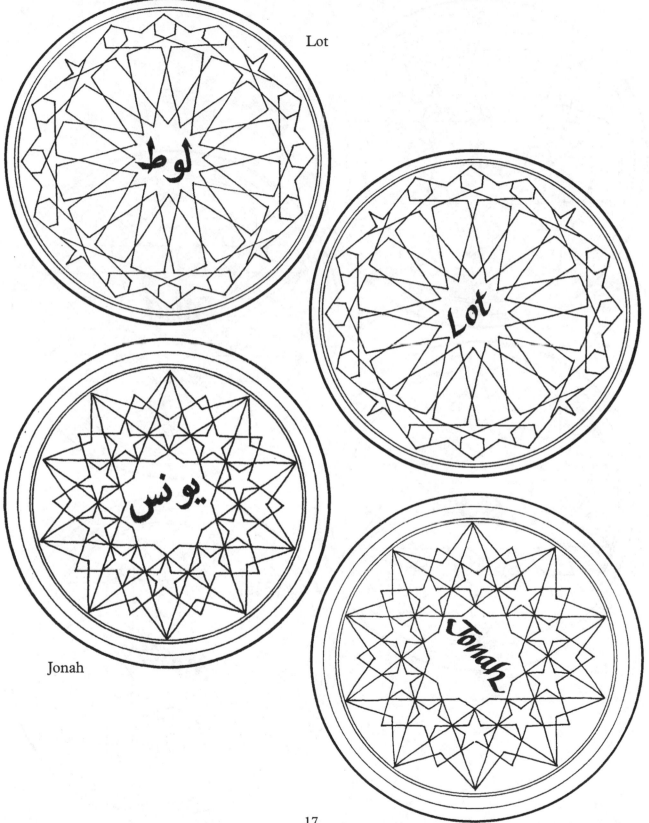

Lot

لوط

Lot

يونس

Jonah

Jonah

17

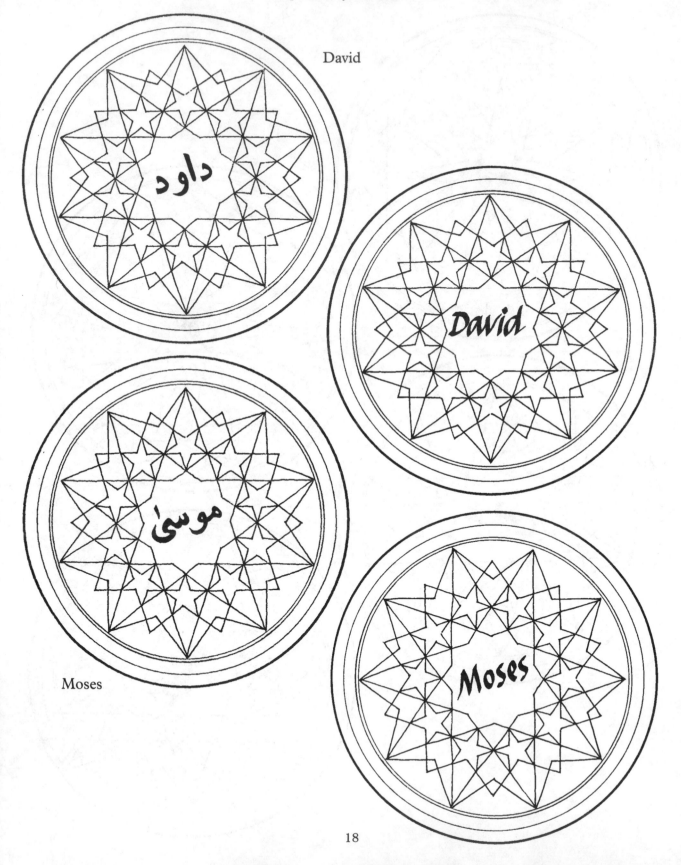

David

داود

David

موسی

Moses

Moses

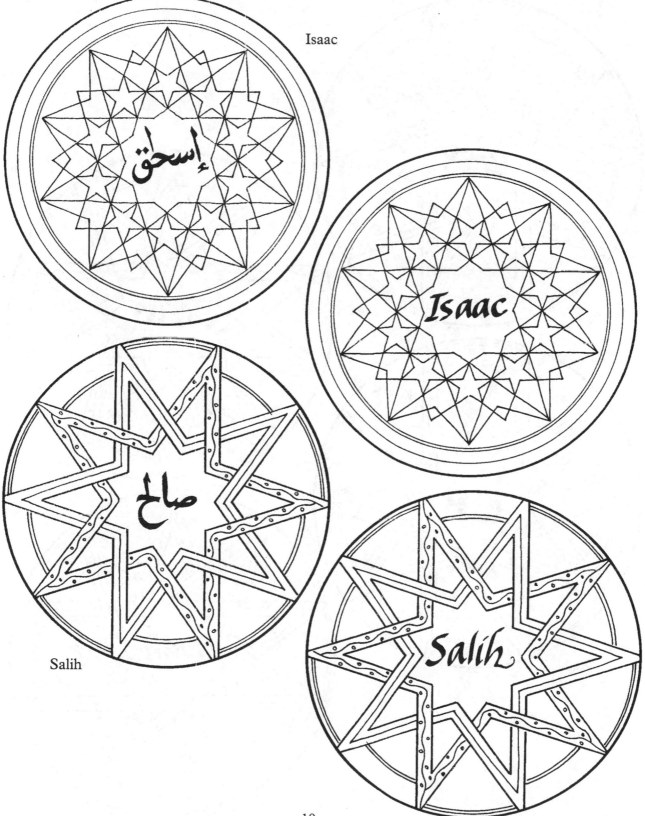

Isaac

إسحق

Isaac

صالح

Salih

Salih

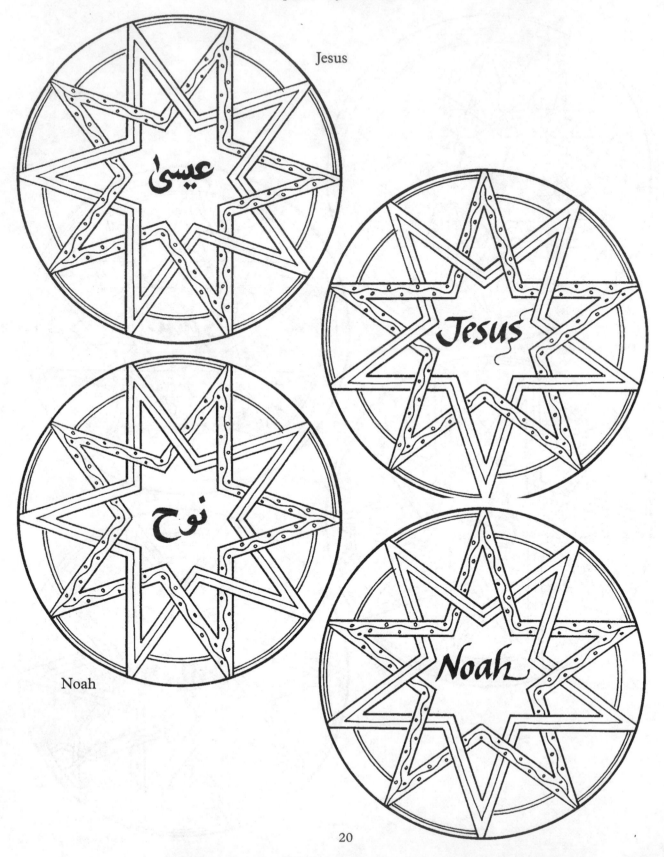

Jesus

Jesus

Noah

Noah

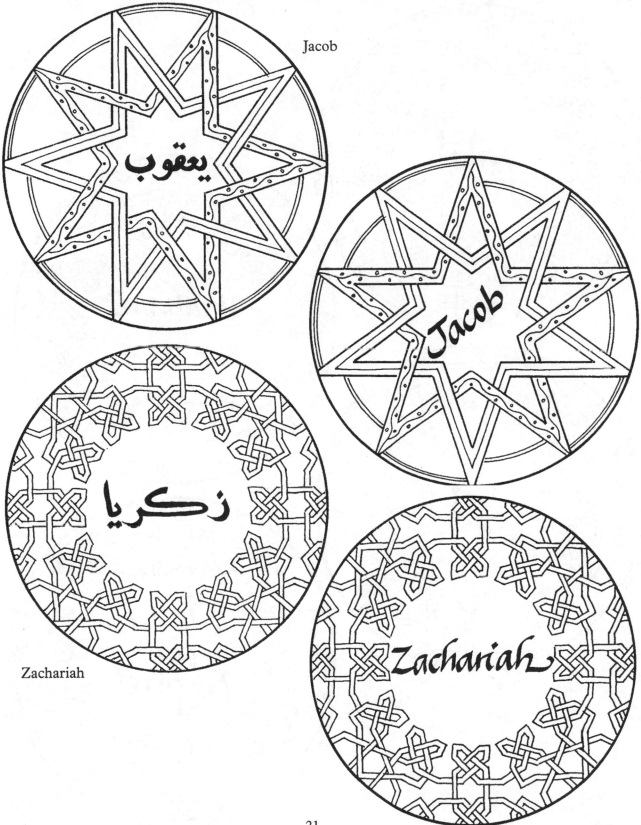

Jacob

يعقوب

Jacob

زكريا

Zachariah

Zachariah

Abraham

إبراهيم

Abraham

يحيى

John the
Baptist

John
the
Baptist

Hud

Muhammad

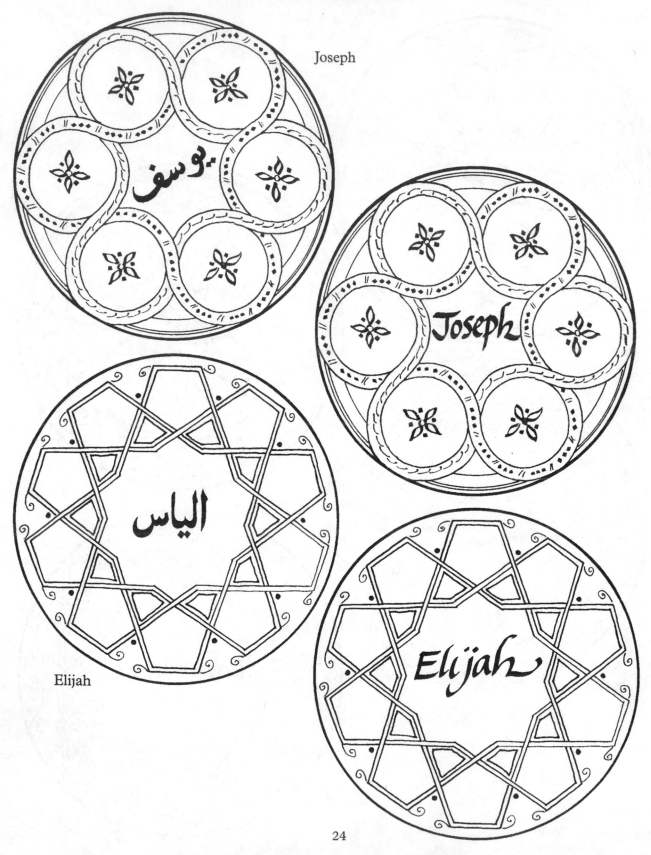

Joseph

Joseph

Elijah

Elijah

Ismail

اسماعيل

Ismail

سليمان

Solomon

Solomon

25

Allah

Allah

ذو الكفل

Ezekiel

Ezekiel

26

Elisha

الیسع

Elisha

شعيب

Shuaib

Shuaib

Activity 3: making a Zakariyya Tray

Materials:

(As many of these as you can, the first 9 items should certainly be present)

Candles, the longer the better

Tray, the larger the better (traditionally, round metal ones are used)

Clay, or Blu-Tack for fixing the candles

Water vessels or small pottery vases

Green leaves and branches

Plain white yoghurt (bio-yoghurt), sweet yoghurts can also be used

Wheat bread

Water from a well (spring water will also do)

Boiled sweets and wrapped sweets, multi-coloured look nicer

Sesame seeds

Raisins and/or sultanas

Nuts including pistachios, walnut, hazelnut, etc.

Dried fruits including any crystallised fruits

Date syrup (dates can substitute for the syrup)

Matches

Safety pins

Setting up:

If you do not have a metal tray, cover a plastic one with tin foil, this will give a nice silver colour, and will be safer when the candles are lit.

1 Position one water vessel in the centre of the tray.

2 Put in it a little water and the green stems and branches.

3 Position candles round the vessel (four candles should be sufficient for a medium sized tray). Make sure that when these

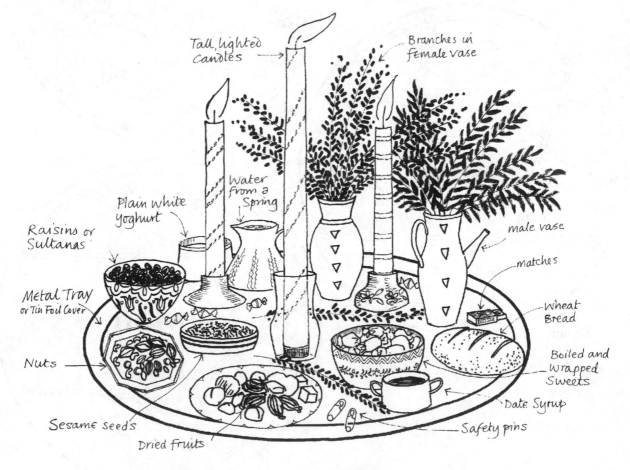

Tall, lighted candles

Branches in female vase

Water from a Spring

Plain white yoghurt

Raisins or Sultanas

male vase

matches

Metal Tray or Tin Foil Cover

Wheat Bread

Nuts

Boiled and Wrapped Sweets

Date Syrup

Sesame seeds

Safety pins

Dried Fruits

candles are lit they will not burn the green branches and leaves near to them.

4 In small saucers or bowls put the raisins, nuts, dates, dried fruits, etc. and position these around and in between the candles.

5 Scatter the boiled sweets on the tray, around all the above.

6 At sunset, invite each person to light a candle, make a wish, and stick a pin in the side of a candle.

7 The sweets and other foodstuffs are for eating.

8 Don't forget to take photos.

Activity 4: cooking Zerdah wa Halib (Iraqi rice pudding)

Ingredients:

For zerdah:
2 cups date syrup (can be obtained from Middle Eastern shops, otherwise you can try other syrups)
$1/2$ cup rice
3 cups water
$1/2$ teaspoon ground cardamom or rosewater
$1/4$ teaspoon salt

For rice pudding:
2 cups whole milk
$1/2$ cup rice
3 cups water
$1/2$ teaspoon ground cardamom or rosewater
$1/4$ teaspoon salt

Method:

For zerdah:
1 Clean rice, wash and soak for 10 minutes in cold water.
2 Boil water in a saucepan; add rice to boiling water and stir occasionally. Add date syrup and continue to stir until sauce is thick and rice is cooked.
3 Pour in dish and leave to cool.

For rice pudding:
1 Clean rice, wash and soak for 10 minutes in cold water.
2 Boil water in a saucepan, add rice, and stir until rice is almost cooked.
3 Add milk and reduce heat. Continue stirring until a thick sauce is obtained, as for the zerdah. Add ground cardamom or rosewater and mix well.
4 Pour into serving dish and serve with the zerdah, in a separate dish.
5 As an alternative, both may be served in the same dish, with the zerdah poured on top of the rice pudding.
6 The rice pudding may be served alone, with the addition of 4 teaspoons sugar while mixture is cooking.

Activity 5: making a small water vessel for the Zakariyya Tray

(Boys make pots with a spout; girls make round neck pots.)

Materials:
A pack of modelling clay. This comes in several colours. If you chose white, you would be able to colour it with any patterns you like. 'DAS Pronto' is a white, air-hardening modelling material, which can be purchased from art materials and equipment shops
Suitable make of colours: ceramic gloss colours can be purchased from art

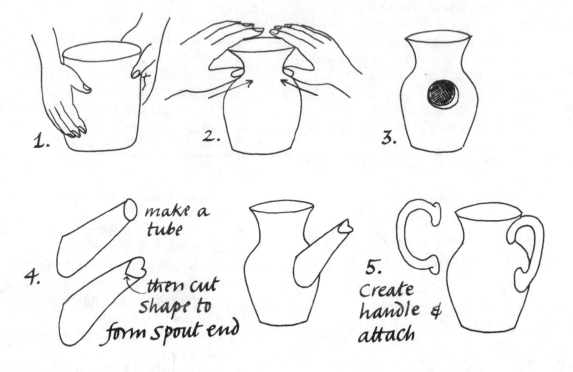

1.

2.

3.

4. make a tube

then cut shape to form spout end

5. Create handle & attach

materials and equipment shops. *'Pebeo'* make a range of cold ceramic colours, and *'Humbrol'* make a range of cold enamel paints, all of which dry without the need for baking

Brushes and thinners for the paints

Rolling pin, knife, and other simple tools to help in shaping the clay

Method:

1 Shape the bowl of the vessel first.
2 Shape the rim of the vessel next.
3 Make a hole for the spout.
4 Shape the spout and attach it to the vessel.
5 Shape the handle and attach to the vessel.
6 Leave to dry. Follow the instructions on the pack.
7 Colour with cheerful colours and designs. You can use Islamic patterns. (See back of book for sample patterns).

Chapter 2

THE BIRTH

O Prophet, we have sent you as a witness, a bearer of glad tidings, and a giver of warnings; and as one who calls people to God by His leave, as a lamp spreading light. Then give the glad tiding to the believers that they shall have from God great bounty. And obey not the unbelievers and the hypocrites, and disregard their insolence. But put your trust in God your guardian.

The Qur'an: *Surat Al-Ahzab*

The Birth of the Prophet

The growth of Makkah

For many centuries the descendants of Ishmael took care of the Sacred House in Makkah, worshipping a single god as Abraham had done. But with time old pagan beliefs resurfaced and the practice of worshipping many gods, in the form of statues and carvings, returned to the city. But throughout this period Makkah and the House of God were still considered holy to the Arabs. People travelled to Makkah from many countries to worship there. The Ka'bah was filled with statues of gods worshipped by pagan tribes. Each tribe would deposit its own statue in the Ka'bah. All this made Makkah a very important pilgrimage city. Makkah also became an economic centre, due to its place on the trade route between Yemen in the South and Syria to the North.

Arabia in the Sixth Century A.D.

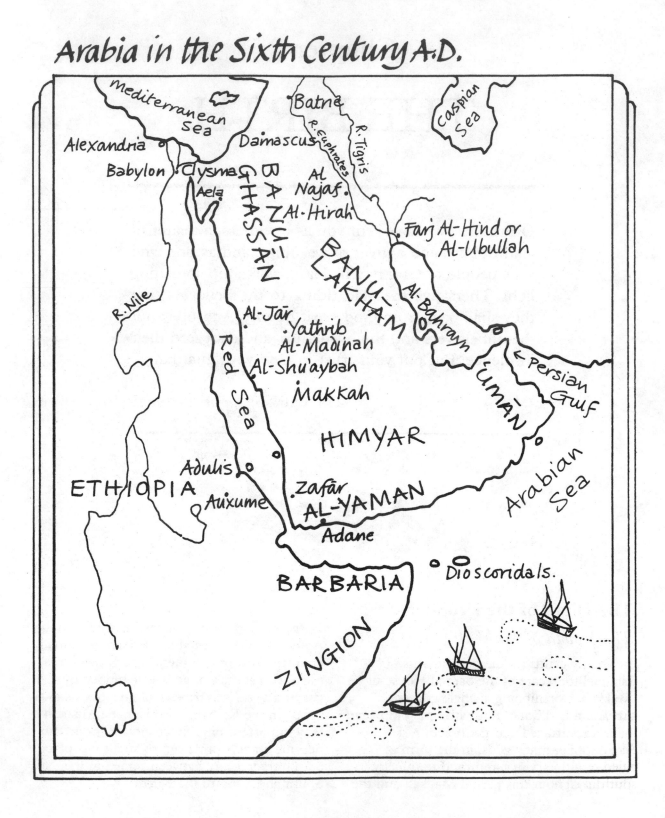

The Year of the Elephant

Long after Abraham had lived, and six
centuries after the birth of Jesus, the Prophet
Muhammad was born in Makkah. At that
time there were three main religions in the
area: Christianity, Judaism and Paganism.
The year of the Prophet's birth is known as
the Year of the Elephant, because of a miracle
that occurred shortly before he was born.

At that time an Ethiopian called Abraha
ruled over the kingdom of Yemen to the
south of Makkah. Abraha was a Christian,

and he built a magnificent cathedral (called
Al-Qulaiss, in Yemen). He wrote to the king
of Ethiopia, saying that even though he had
built the cathedral in the king's honour, the
Arabs still made pilgrimage to Makkah and
did not worship in the cathedral. Abraha told
the king that he wanted to change this and
persuade the Arabs to worship in the new
cathedral.

A pagan Arab from Makkah heard about this
letter, and was angry that Abraha should
challenge Makkah and the Sacred House in
this way. The man travelled to Yemen, went

to the cathedral, and insulted it in the worst way he could imagine. He went to the toilet inside the cathedral! Soon after this the man returned to Makkah.

When Abraha heard about this he was furious. He decided to go to Makkah in order to destroy the Sacred House. Preparations were made and Abraha set out for Makkah at the head of a vast army led by a long column of soldiers riding African elephants. On the route to Makkah all who tried to oppose the army were easily defeated, and their leaders taken captive.

Abu Rughal's betrayal of the sacred house

During Abraha's journey to Makkah, an Arab villager, Abu Rughal, was taken captive. He showed Abraha the route across the desert to Makkah and died on the journey. Today Muslims commemorate this betrayal by throwing stones at his grave as part of their pilgrimage to Makkah, at a place called Al-Mghmas.

Abraha and Abd Al-Mutalib

Abraha's army was soon at the edge of Makkah. The first thing they did there was steal all the herds of the Makkah tribes, including 200 camels belonging to Abd Al-Mutalib, the chief of a tribe called the Quraish. The Quraish were in charge of taking care of the Sacred House in Makkah, and were a powerful and important family there. Abraha sent a messenger to Abd Al-Mutalib, saying:

'I have not come to Makkah to conquer you, but only to destroy the Sacred House. Let me do this, and your people will not be harmed.'

Al-Mutalib sent back the message, 'We have no wish to fight as we are no match for your forces.'

When Abraha received this message he invited Al-Mutalib to visit his camp. When Al-Mutalib arrived, Abraha was impressed by the calm and dignity of the leader. When asked why he had come, Al-Mutalib replied, 'I wish you to return to me the camels you have stolen.'

This answer surprised Abraha, who replied, 'Why do you only ask for this, when my army has come to destroy the Sacred House which your family has protected for thousands of years?'

Al-Mutalib replied, 'I defend the camels, as they are mine. But the Sacred House has a far mightier owner than me, and he will defend it when needed.'

'The Lord of the House will not be able to stop me knocking it down,' boasted Abraha.

'That,' replied Al-Mutalib, 'is between you and Him!'

Abraha was surprised and puzzled by this answer. He gave Al-Mutalib back his camels and allowed him to return home.

When Al-Mutalib reached Makkah, he ordered all of the citizens to leave the city and hide in caves in the nearby mountains. They did this, leaving only Al-Mutalib and a few other leaders to stay behind at the Sacred House.

The army advanced, unopposed, towards Makkah, with Abraha leading the way on his great elephant, Mahmood. As they approached the empty city, one of the Arab leaders who had been captured on the route to Makkah whispered in the elephant's ear:

'Kneel down, sit, or return from where you came. You are in God's Holy Land.'

The elephant stopped, knelt down and would not go any further. They pulled him, beat him and stabbed him with iron spikes, but the great elephant would not take a single step in the direction of Makkah. But as soon as his head was turned away from Makkah he happily started walking back toward Yemen.

At that moment, thousands of strange birds filled the sky: sea swallows and starlings from the Red Sea. Each bird held three tiny stones, one in their beaks and one in each of their claws. The birds hovered high above the army and started dropping the stones on the soldiers' heads. The stones killed the men just by touching them. Abraha and many of his soldiers were killed. Those who survived ran back to Yemen.

The birth and early life of the Prophet

Soon after this miracle, the prophet Muhammad, the grandson of Abd Al-Mutalib, was born in Makkah. It was 570 AD. His parents were from the Quraish tribe, in charge of taking care of the House of God.

His early years were marked by a series of deaths amongst his close family. Muhammad's father, Abd Allah, had died before Muhammad was born. His mother, Amina, died when he was six years old, and Muhammad was then looked after by Abd Al-Mutalib, his grandfather. Two years later his grandfather died, and his care passed on to his uncle, Abu Talib.

Muhammad spent much of his childhood working as a goatherd, taking care of his uncle's flocks. He also accompanied his uncle on trading visits to Syria.

Even before he became a prophet, Muhammad had such a good reputation for honesty and wisdom that he was known as 'the trustworthy one' within his own community. For example, once Muhammad's tribe decided to rebuild the walls of the sacred house. When it was time to replace the sacred black stone in one corner of the House, a dispute broke out between four of the tribes about which should have the honour of putting the stone in place. Muhammad was asked to intervene in the dispute, and asked them to spread a black cloak on the ground and place the stone at its centre. Each of the clan leaders took one of the four corners of the cloak, lifted the stone together, and so shared the honour of replacing the stone.

When he was 25 years old, Muhammad was married. His wife Khadijah was 15 years older than her husband. The couple were happily married and had several children.

As the years went by Muhammad became more and more interested in the religious life. At that time it was the custom to spend the month of Ramadan fasting and praying. During this month he would spend periods in solitude and prayer, in a mountain cave near to Makkah.

The Prophet's Birthday

The Prophet Muhammad was born on a Monday, on the 12th of the month of Rabea Al-Awal. (This was 570 AD during the month of August according to the Christian calendar). His name means 'the praised or the praiseworthy in heaven and on earth'.

Muhammad's birth signified a new dawn for the Arabs in particular, and those who would become Muslims in general. Muhammad's life, prophet-hood, and achievements gave rise to a new civilization that dominated large parts of the old world between 750 AD and 1258 AD.

Muhammad called for worshipping the One God, the God of heaven and earth. He called people to lead good lives, avoid evil, and spread the Word of God. As the 'Messenger', Muhammad's duty lay in delivering the Qur'an, revealed to him by the Archangel Gabriel, who was instructed by God. As the Prophet, Muhammad's duty was to lead his followers, giving a good example of the right way to live.

Celebrating the Prophet's birth (Milad-an-Nabi, or Al-Mawlood)

The Birth of the Prophet Muhammad is celebrated, on the 12th of Rabea Al-Awal (the third month of the Muslim year – see Chapter 3 for discussion of the Muslim calendar).

Celebrations usually take place in the evening. People go to the mosque to pray and attend the religious festivities. In some countries this includes religious chanting accompanied by drums. The chanters sing the praises of the Prophet Muhammad. The worshippers may join in as well.

As it is not customary for women to go to the mosque very often, the women of the family often celebrate Milad-an-Nabi at home. In some countries, professional Mawlood singers can be hired to sing for the family gathering.

Whether in the mosque or at home, an evening meal is served to all who attend.

Celebrating the Prophet's birthday in Egypt

Ask any Arabs about the Milad-an-Nabi, and they will tell you that no one celebrates the Prophet's birthday like the Egyptians. It is a truly exciting time, especially for children. All the mosques are celebrating. And in Cairo each local district has its own celebrations. The streets are decorated with chains of coloured flags and lanterns. There are traditional fun fairs for children, with wooden swings and wheels. All the food and sweets shops stay open until midnight, and street sellers are out and about with their wares.

In Egypt children are given small coloured lanterns to carry around the streets during these evening celebrations. Such lanterns are usually made of metal frames and coloured glass sheets, containing a lit candle.

For the celebration to be complete, every child has to have a sugar doll or horse – dolls for girls, and horses for boys. Traditional

sweet shops, or 'Halawani', make these dolls and horses. They are coloured and dressed in colourful paper clothes and saddles.

Celebrating the Prophet's birthday in Iraq

In Baghdad, people usually go to one of two large mosques in the city for the prayers and commemoration events. Candles are lit in the courtyards of these mosques. Inside the mosque, helpers distribute and sprinkle rosewater on the congregation. As they wipe their hands and face with rosewater they seek God's blessings. The Qur'an is recited; praise, tribute and commendation of the Prophet Muhammad's life and deeds are spoken and sung, aided by tambourines. Prayers are spoken together.

At home, people fast during the day, prepare food for the break-fast at sunset, and light candles for this occasion.

Activity Ideas

✦ Drawing and colouring an elephant

✦ Making a candle lantern

✦ Making a model horse or doll

✦ Cooking konafa with cheese (a traditional sweet dish)

Activity 1: drawing and colouring an elephant

After hearing the story of Mahmood the elephant, why not draw some scenes from the story? Elephants have been used throughout history in many battles and campaigns. Children might like to draw and colour an elephant in the service of the army.

Choose one of the
Elephants on this
page to copy,
enlarge and colour.

Activity 2: making a candle lantern

CAUTION

Candles must not be lit without the supervision of an adult. This lamp is designed to hold a small tea-light candle only. They must be fitted into their aluminium holders.

Materials:

White card (200g minimum)

Transparent plastic sheets (overhead projector sheets, especially those suitable for use in photocopying machines, can be bought from any good stationery suppliers). Recycling the covers of plastic folders is an alternative

Stained glass colours (transparent water based ones, made by 'Pebeo' etc. can be purchased from art materials suppliers, or from children's centres)

Brush

Glue

Scissors and cutter (stencil knife)

Ruler

Pencil

Colouring pens, pencils, or pastels

Ball-point pen

Metal chain, or strong fibre string (200cm or 79 inches)

Hole-puncher

Two small metal rings (similar to the kind used in key-rings)

Blu-Tack or similar

Method:

1 Cut out base of lamp.
2 Cut out sides of lamp in one strip.
3 Using the cutter (stencil knife) cut out the arches.
4 Colour the frames on one side, the outside, using the pens, pencils, or pastels.
5 Cut transparent rectangles to fit the frames and cover the arches.
6 Colour the transparent sheets using the stained glass transparent colours and leave to dry for the recommended time.
7 When dry, stick the transparent sheets in the frames to cover the arches, making sure you stick them to the inside of the frames and not the coloured outside surface.
8 Fold the sides of the frames along the dividing lines, to make the 8-sided shape that should fit the base of the lamp.
9 Glue the two sides of the frames together.
10 Glue the frames to the base.
11 Using the hole-puncher, make 4 holes on the top edge of the lamp, at equal distances, on every other side.
12 Cut two 60cm (24 inches) pieces of the chain or string.
13 Link/tie each end of each string in the two opposite holes, so that the two strings cross each other.
14 Using one metal ring, join the two chains/strings together.
15 Attach a length of 20cm (8 inches) of the chain/string to the ring, making a 10cm loop to serve as a handle.
16 Thread the second metal ring through this 20cm piece.
17 Attach the two ends of this chain/string to the first ring.
18 Position a tea-light in the lantern. You can fix it in place with Blu-Tack if needed.
19 Ask an adult to light it for you.
20 Under the supervision of an adult, you can walk about with this lantern as Egyptian children do during the Milad-an-Nabi Festival.

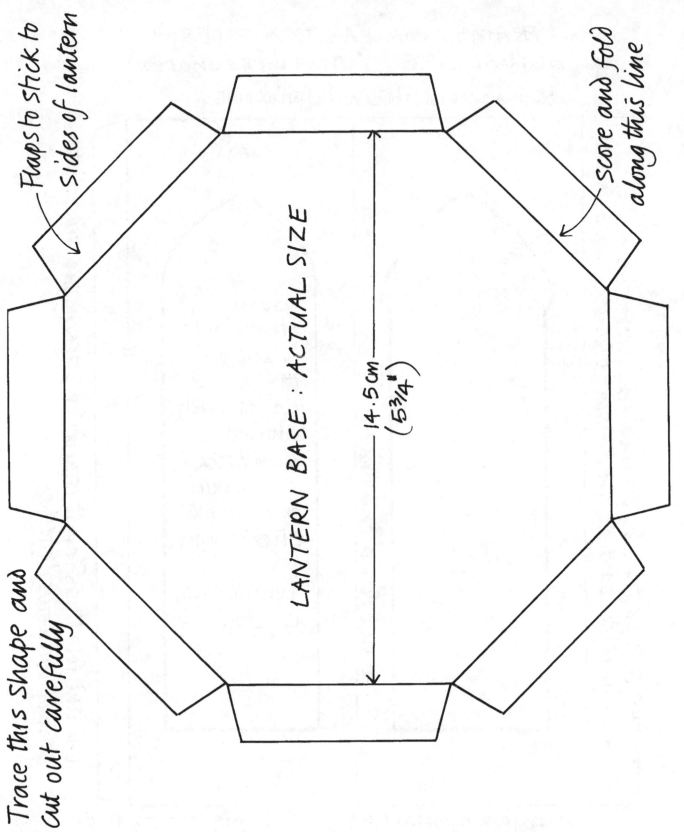

Flaps to stick to sides of lantern

Score and fold along this line

LANTERN BASE : ACTUAL SIZE

14.5cm (5¾")

Trace this shape and cut out carefully

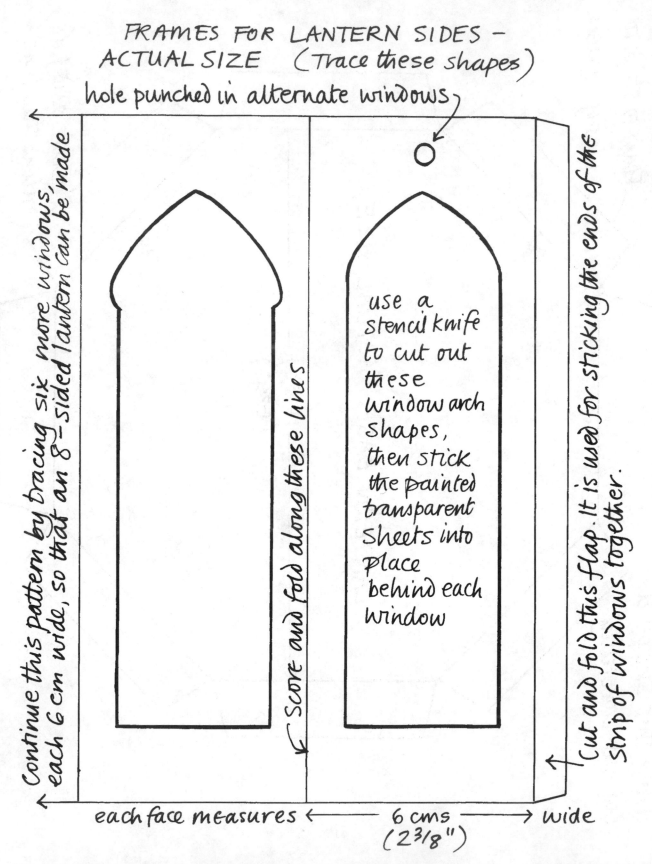

FRAMES FOR LANTERN SIDES —
ACTUAL SIZE (Trace these shapes)

hole punched in alternate windows

Continue this pattern by tracing six more windows, each 6 cm wide, so that an 8-sided lantern can be made

Score and fold along these lines

use a stencil knife to cut out these window arch shapes, then stick the painted transparent sheets into place behind each window

Cut and fold this flap. It is used for sticking the ends of the strip of windows together.

each face measures ← 6 cms → wide
(2 3/8")

2) Cut out sides of lantern in one strip

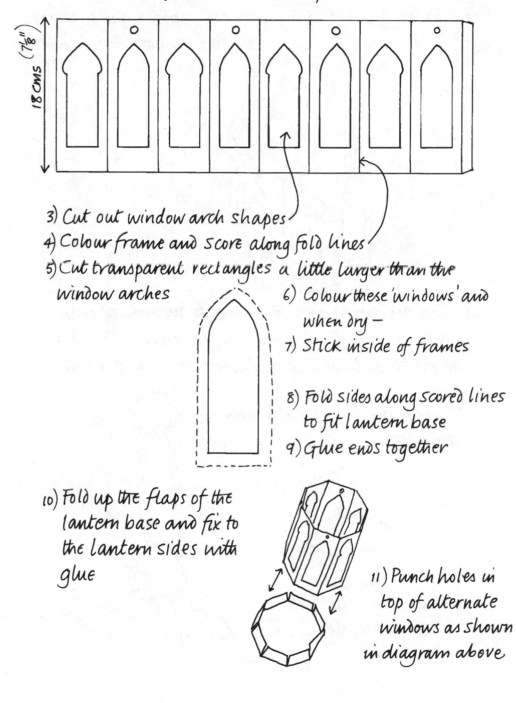

18 CMS (7⅛")

3) Cut out window arch shapes

4) Colour frame and score along fold lines

5) Cut transparent rectangles a little larger than the window arches

6) Colour these 'windows' and when dry —

7) Stick inside of frames

8) Fold sides along scored lines to fit lantern base

9) Glue ends together

10) Fold up the flaps of the lantern base and fix to the lantern sides with glue

11) Punch holes in top of alternate windows as shown in diagram above

12) Cut two 60 cm (24") long pieces of chain, cord or string
13) Link each end of string in the two opposite holes so that the two strings cross each other.

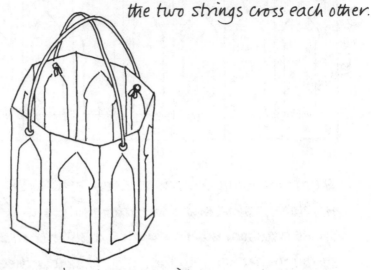

14) Join the two strings together with the metal ring
15) Attach a length of 20 cm (8") of string to the ring to make a 10 cm loop which will serve as a handle

16) Thread the second metal ring → through this loop piece

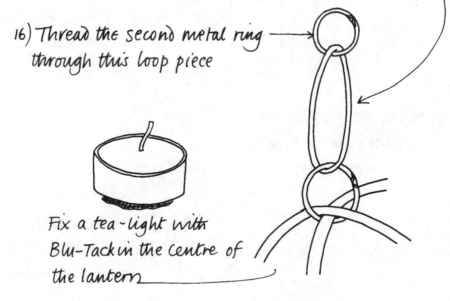

Fix a tea-light with Blu-Tack in the centre of the lantern

Activity 3: making a model horse or doll

Materials:
Although traditional Mawlood dolls and horses are made of sugar and edible, why not try to make one of these using modelling clay? This clay comes in several colours. Choose white, so that you are able to colour it and glue coloured paper on it, just like the 'Halawani' does when preparing a traditional Mawlood sugar doll or horse. 'DAS Pronto' is a white air-hardening modelling material, which can be purchased from art materials and equipment shops.

Coloured paper. You can recycle silver paper from chocolate bars and cigarette boxes, as the 'Halawani' does
Colours suitable for painting on modelling clay
Glue, brush, scissors

Method:
1 Shape the clay into the doll or horse.
2 Leave to dry thoroughly.
3 Draw and colour the face.
4 Cut out the clothes and saddle from the collection of coloured paper.
5 Don't forget to make an appropriate head-dress.
6 Stick everything on.

(see diagrams on following 2 pages)

Activity 4: cooking konafa with cheese (a traditional sweet dish)

This sweet dish is a favourite in the Middle East. It is eaten at festivals and celebrations in Palestine, Syria, Jordan, and Iraq.

Ingredients:
1 bag of fresh vermicelli (konafa)
1 packet of white cheese (not salted)
Butter to grease the baking tray
Sugar syrup. If you want to do your own syrup you will need:
   $1/2$ kg sugar
   300 ml water
1 tablespoon lemon juice
2 tablespoons rosewater or orange flower water

Method:
1 In a buttered oven tray spread half the quantity of vermicelli.
2 Grate or finely cut the cheese, and spread over the vermicelli.
3 Add the second half of the vermicelli on top of the cheese, and press down firmly and evenly.
4 Oven bake on medium heat for $3/4$ to 1 hour, until the vermicelli is cooked and becomes golden in colour on the surface.
5 Prepare the sugar syrup by dissolving the sugar in the water on the stove, stirring it until all is dissolved. Add the lemon juice and rosewater; and leave to cool.
6 Take out of the oven, and pour the cooled thin sugar syrup all over it.
7 Serve while still hot.

1. Make head, neck, body, arms and legs. Shape clay into doll figure

OR

Make head, ears, neck, body and legs of horse

2. Leave to dry

3. Define and colour facial features

4. Cut out the clothes & saddle from the collection of coloured papers

5. Make an appropriate head-dress for the doll

Attach head-dress
to doll's head
like a crown

Make a
small-bead
necklace

Use sequins and
coloured cut-
out shapes
on crêpe
paper for
doll's skirt.
Use silver and gold
papers and
decorations,
also for saddle.
Try straw for tail

Cut stiff paper
&
and attach to
horse's neck as
a mane

Stories of Obedience

On the Prophet's birthday his life and teachings are remembered and celebrated. One of the main teachings is the notion of obedience to the will of God, and the consequences of disobedience – as shown, for example, in the story of Abraha. Here are a few folktales from Islamic countries that explore this theme from different points of view.

Juha God Willing

This story is about a popular character throughout the Islamic world called Juha. Juha is a character who is sometimes foolish, sometimes wise, and sometimes both at the same time! His tales are very well known in the Islamic world. They may be treated as jokes, as fables or as deep religious teachings: religious sects use the stories as objects of meditation.

Muslims often use the phrase 'Insh'allah', meaning 'God willing', when talking about the future, to remind them that ultimately it is God's will, rather than their own personal wishes, which is important.

For example a Muslim may say: 'See you tomorrow, insh'allah', or 'Tomorrow insh'allah, I will go to the market.'

A newsreader on TV might say: 'This time tomorrow we will be back, insh'allah.' A bus driver may shout out 'To Aleppo, insh'allah!'

This first story is told in many Islamic countries, and illustrates the importance attached to the idea of God's will in Islam. This particular version was collected in Palestine.

Once there was a man called Juha, who lived in a cottage a long way from the nearest town. When the weather was fine he worked in his fields. When the weather was bad he worked in his workshop. He never said insh'allah, which worried his wife.

One night he said to his wife:

'Wife, pack my bag with food tomorrow and check the bags of seeds. It looks like the weather is clearing. Tomorrow I will finish sowing the fields with wheat. I want to start early, so please get everything ready tonight.'

'Let's wait and see,' said his wife, 'Nobody knows what tomorrow may bring.'

'I know what tomorrow will bring,' replied Juha. 'If it is fine I will sow, and if it rains I will work at home making a new plough. Those are my plans, and that's what will happen.'

The farmer's wife waggled her finger at him. 'Husband, you should say insh'allah. Please say insh'allah. Nobody knows what will happen tomorrow but God!'

Juha paid no attention to his wife, who got things ready for the next day, baking fresh bread and preparing the seeds for sowing.

The next morning the couple were woken up by a knock on the door. When Juha opened the door a face scowled down at him. It was a soldier.

'Show me the way to town,' ordered the soldier.

'Well, you go down this road, first on the left, second on the right and then straight on till a fork in the road where you turn right and …'

'No need to tell me. Take me there, show me the way yourself!' he shouted.

'But…I can't take you there. It's three hours' walk, and today I have to sow my fields,' pleaded Juha.

The soldier, who was not used to having his orders questioned, took Juha by the scruff of the neck and gave him three sharp knocks

Chapter 2 The Birth

on the head. Juha had no choice but to walk for three long hours with the soldier to town, and another three hours back in the heat of the midday sun.

When he returned, tired, hungry and thirsty, he found the door of his house locked. His wife had locked it, fearing the return of another soldier.

'Who is it?' she called through the door.

'It's Juha insh'allah. Please let me in! It's Juha insh'allah! It's Juha God willing!'

The Unlucky Man

This is a story from Uzbekistan, although similar tales can be found all over the world.

Once there was a man, called Ahmed, who thought himself unlucky. While everyone else seemed to have good luck, all his own luck seemed to be only bad, or at least that was how he saw it. He asked many people why his luck was so bad, but nobody

could tell him. Many said that only God could give him the answer. Eventually Ahmed decided to pay God a visit, at the top of the sacred mountain, to ask about his luck.

Ahmed travelled to the foothills of the mountain, and started walking up the mountain path. After a day or so he came to a wolf lying by the side of the path. The wolf looked thin and ill. As Ahmed hurried past the wolf, the animal called out:

'Excuse me sir, where are you going in such a hurry?'

'I'm going to ask God why I don't have any luck' replied Ahmed.

'Well, when you see him, could you please ask him from me why I am so thin and weak, and what I should do about it?' said the wolf.

'Yes, I'll ask him,' said Ahmed, and continued on his way up the mountain.

Ahmed climbed for another day, and came to a thin tiny tree growing by the side of the path. As the man walked by, the tree spoke:

'Excuse me sir, where are you going in such a hurry?'

'I'm going to ask God why I don't have any luck.' replied Ahmed.

'Look around you,' replied God, compassionately. 'Luck is all around you! Find it and take it. Do as I tell you and all will be well.'

'Thanks, I'll go home and look for my luck.'

Ahmed was about to leave when he remembered the questions of the wolf, the tree and the woman. He asked the questions and God told him the answers. As soon as God had finished, Ahmed rushed off down the mountain, keen to go home and start looking for his luck.

He walked briskly down the mountain for a day and a night and a night and a day until he came to the cottage. The pretty young woman called out to him from the doorway

'Did you get an answer to my question?'

'Well when you see him, could you please ask him from me why I am so thin and small, and what I should do about it?' asked the tree.

'Yes, I'll ask him,' replied Ahmed, and continued on his way up the mountain.

Ahmed climbed for another day until he came to a cottage by the side of the path, with a beautiful young women standing in the doorway. She called out to the man as he hurried by:

'Excuse me sir, where are you going in such a hurry?'

'I'm going to ask God why I don't have any luck,' replied Ahmed.

'Well when you see him, could you please ask him from me why I am so lonely, and what I should do about it?' said the young woman.

'Yes, I'll ask him,' said Ahmed, and continued on his way up the mountain.

Ahmed walked up the mountain for a day and a night and a night and a day until, finally, he came to the mountaintop where God was waiting for him.

'God, please tell me why I don't have any luck. How can I find my luck?'

'Yes,' said Ahmed, 'God said you should get married. Find yourself a husband and then you won't be lonely.'

The girl gave Ahmed a long hard look and said 'Well, will you marry me then?'

'Sorry,' said Ahmed, 'I haven't got time. I have to go home to look for my luck.' Without giving the matter another thought he rushed off down the mountain.

A while later he came to the small thin tree.

'Did you get an answer to my question?' asked the tree.

'Yes,' said Ahmed, 'God said there is a box of treasure buried under your roots which stops them growing. Get someone to dig it up and you will grow tall and strong.'

'Will *you* dig the box out please,' asked the tree.

'Sorry, but I haven't got time. I need to get home to look for my luck!' replied Ahmed as he hurried off down the mountain.

A good while later Ahmed came to the thin old wolf.

'Did you get an answer to my question?' asked the wolf.

'Yes,' said Ahmed, 'God said that you should eat the first fool who comes along the path.

So the wolf did just that.

The Wishing Cup

This folktale was collected in Kashmir, but its like is found throughout the world in one form or another.

Once, in a small village next to a large forest, lived a man called Kailash. Kailash was very poor and had no work. He was so poor there was nothing to eat in his house. It made Kailash so sad to see his wife thin and starving.

One day he walked out of the village and sat under a tree in the forest. He thought of his wife's thin, sad face and called out:

'Why, God, did you make me so poor that I cannot even feed my own wife? Why? She prays to you every day and never complains. Have pity and help her!'

At that moment Kailash heard footsteps on the path. An old man wearing the robes of a monk came walking along the path leading a donkey by its bridle. The old man stopped in front of Kailash.

'What's the matter, my son? Why do you look so sad?' asked the monk.

'It's no use,' replied Kailash 'nobody can help me!'

'Tell me anyway,' said the monk. 'You never know!'

'I am poor, and my family is starving,' wailed Kailash 'and I can see no way out.'

'Really,' replied the holy man. 'Let me give you a cup.'

'What good is a cup?'

'This is a wishing cup. Wish for something and it will appear.'

The old man took a small cup from his saddlebag and gave it to Kailash, and then continued along the path.

Kailash couldn't believe his luck. He wished for his favourite dish of meat and rice, and it appeared in front of him on a fine metal plate. It looked delicious. It smelled

even better! Kailash ate hungrily till his belly was full and satisfied.

On his way home, Kailash passed by the hut of a very poor family. A mother lived there with five hungry children. Her husband had died recently and now they lived by begging. Kailash heard the children crying that they were too hungry to sleep, and their mother told them that, God willing, tomorrow she would find them some food.

Kailash knocked on the door of the hut, and when the mother answered he said:

'I couldn't help overhearing how hungry your children are. Would you allow me to give them a meal, as a gift?'

The woman smiled and invited Kailash into her house. He sat down with the family around him, took out his cup, and wished for six plates of food. The food appeared instantly in front of them and Kailash watched happily as the hungry family filled their bellies.

The children's mother, however, had her eyes on the magic cup. While Kailash was watching her children eating, she took the cup, replacing it with one of her own, ordinary cups. Kailash noticed nothing, took the other cup and went home.

When he reached his own hut he called to his wife,

'Come and see! Wife, come and see!'

When his wife saw Kailash holding up the cup her face fell.

'What's so important about an old cup?' she asked.

'But wife, this is no ordinary cup. This one has magic powers. Just take it and wish for whatever food you like, and the food will appear.'

His wife gave Kailash a look as if to say he had gone mad. She took the cup and wished and wished, but nothing happened. Kailash took the cup back and wished, but again nothing happened. His wife burst out crying, even more hungry now after imagining so much delicious food.

The next day Kailash went back into the forest to the same tree where he had met the monk. After a while the monk turned up again.

'What are you doing here this time?' asked the monk.

'The cup you gave me doesn't work anymore,' answered Kailash.

'Show it to me' said the monk, and when Kailash showed him the cup the man first laughed and then frowned.

'This is not the cup I gave you,' he said sternly. 'Are you trying to trick me and get two cups?'

'No, sir, not at all,' protested Kailash.

'Well tell me everything that happened since you took the cup.'

Kailash told him everything and when he had finished the old man said:

'The old woman must have taken your cup and replaced it with another. Here, take this second cup and give it to the woman, and ask her to wish for anything she wants.'

Kailash did as the old man had suggested, took the second cup and returned to the family a second time. The children rushed out to welcome him. The woman was frightened he had come back to accuse her, but when Kailash explained he had brought a second cup for her to wish with, she smiled and took the cup, closed her eyes and made a wish.

The next moment two big sticks popped out of the cup and started beating the woman. She ran and tried to get away under the bed, but the sticks followed her there and kept beating till she cried out 'Please, take the cup away. I am sorry. I'll give you the one I took yesterday.'

Kailash picked up the cup, and when he covered it with his hands, the sticks disappeared. When the woman handed him the wishing cup Kailash said he would return every day to give the children food, then he rushed back home to his wife. They had the finest feast of all their lives, and lived happily ever after.

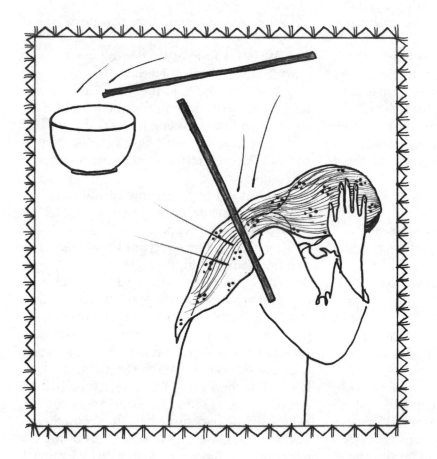

Chapter 3

PROPHETHOOD BEGINS

We have revealed [the Qur'an] in the Night of Destiny.
But how would you know what the Night of Destiny is?
The Night of Destiny is better than a thousand months.
Therein come down the angels and the Holy Spirit by
God's permission, on every errand. Peace is this Night
until the break of dawn.

The Qur'an: *Surat Al-Qadr*

The First Vision

We have heard how Muhammad was born in the holy city of Makkah, where he was raised by his grandfather after his mother died, and later by his uncle. As he grew older he gained a reputation for wisdom and fairness, and became more interested in religious life.

When Muhammad was forty years old, he was meditating one night in a cave near Makkah. It was the month of Ramadan, when it was the custom to fast and pray. During this month Muhammad would spend long periods alone in the cave. One night an angel appeared to him and commanded him to read. Muhammad was terrified, and did not understand the command.

'I cannot read!' he protested, as he had never learned either to read or write.

'Read!' the angel commanded again, this time so fiercely that the earth seemed to shake under him. Again he protested that he could not.

A third time the angel repeated his command, and this time Muhammad replied differently.

'What shall I read?' he asked.

At that moment space and time were suspended, and the angel spoke the first verses of what was to become the holy Qur'an:

'Read!
In the name of the Lord who creates man from a clot of blood.
Read!
Your Lord is most generous.
He taught men through the pen what was not known before.'

When this first vision had passed, Muhammad was frightened. He did not understand what had happened and was scared that he might be going mad. Muhammad hurried to his wife, Khadijah. He told her about the vision, and said he was frightened that something bad might be happening to him. Khadijah comforted her husband, telling him to have courage and be glad about what had happened.

Khadijah knew a wise old scholar called Waraqa, who lived in Makkah at that time. She went to him and explained what had happened to her husband. When he heard the details he was amazed, and told Khadijah that her husband must be the Prophet who had been mentioned in the old scriptures.

'Oh most Holy God,' he cried, 'If what you say is true then a great angel has come to Muhammad, just as he came before Moses. Muhammad will be the prophet of the nation. Tell him to have courage and faith!'

When Khadijah returned home Muhammad was sleeping, huddled under a pile of blankets. As she watched him he started to sweat and shake as Gabriel spoke to him a second time:

'Shake off those things that cover you!' called the angel, 'and bring God's message to his people.'

When Muhammad woke up, Khadijah explained what Waraqa had said, and encouraged him to have faith in his vision. In this way the work of the Prophet started. The night of his first revelation is celebrated during the last ten days of the month of Ramadan, and is known as Laylat-ul-Qadr, the Night of Destiny.

A few days later Waraqa met Muhammad at the House of God (see chapter 1), and asked him to describe again what had happened in the cave. When he had heard the story he told Muhammad that he would be the new prophet of the nation, but that he would be fought, ridiculed and exiled by those who would not accept the teaching. He promised to support the Prophet and kissed his forehead as a sign of respect.

Muhammad continued to experience revelations during periods of solitude in the cave, passing on the teachings first to family and friends, some of whom believed in him, while others did not. Slowly the number of his followers grew.

Then, in one revelation, Muhammad was commanded to deliver the message of Islam to the general public. He began to speak in public, teaching that there was only one, universal God, and that he was the messenger of that God. These sacred words became the first of five 'pillars' of Islam, known as the 'Shahadah' or witnessing of belief. Today Muslims affirm their faith by repeating the sacred words:

'In the name of God the compassionate, the merciful
I bear witness that there is no God but Allah
I bear witness that Muhammad is his messenger.'

At first Muhammad's public preaching met with a few converts and much resistance. He was ridiculed and accused of going mad by his townspeople, but not once did Muhammad condemn them. Rather, he said, 'He who believes in God and the day of judgement should either say what is good, or else keep silent.'

One of the things which impressed people about Muhammad's preaching was the beautiful, poetic language which he used to describe his revelations. Muhammad had never composed a poem in his life, yet now he was able to speak in poems of amazing beauty. This strengthened his followers' faith that his words had come from God.

The Night of Destiny (Laylat-ul-Qadr)

This night is normally celebrated on the 27th of Ramadan, during the month of fasting (see chapter 6). It is celebrated all over the Muslim world as the night when the first verses of the Qur'an were revealed to the Prophet (see chapter 3): a time to celebrate the Prophet's message.

The Night of Destiny it considered a special and holy time: a good time for prayers to be answered. It is believed that all the good deeds done on this night earn special merit, as if they were the 'good deeds of a thousand months of labour'. In many countries Muslims stay awake all night, reading the Qur'an, praying, going to the mosques. It is also a time to make peace with any people who have been hurt or offended, and for settling any disputes.

The night is described in the Qur'an with these verses:

We have indeed revealed this in the Night of Destiny.
And what will explain to [Muhammad] what the Night of Destiny is?
The Night of Destiny is better than a thousand months.
On that night the angels and spirits came down by God's permission, each with a decree.
Peace is this night, until the break of dawn.

A Muslim from Bangladesh described this special night with a modern metaphor:

'It's like the night of the budget, when what is planned for the future is revealed!'

Muslims believe that the Qur'an reveals God's plans for the world. It is a special night for prayers. Some choose to pray all through the night on that day. It is an auspicious night for repentance and forgiveness.'

The Qur'an

After the first revelation, the Angel Gabriel continued to visit Muhammad over a period of 23 years. The full collection of revelations makes up the Qur'an (meaning the reading or the book). The Qur'an was revealed in Muhammad's language, Arabic. It has since been translated into all the languages of the world.

The Qur'an contains 114 chapters. 90 chapters were revealed to the Prophet while he was still living in Makkah. The other 24 chapters were revealed to him after moving to Madinah (often spelled Medina) (see chapter 6).

The Qur'an covers all aspects of life: the creation of life and the role of God, personal moral values, laws of civil society and family life, including crime and punishment, marriage and divorce, inheritance, etc. It also tells the stories of the prophets and other parables.

What was Muhammad called to do?

Muslims believe that God chose Muhammad to deliver his message (the Qur'an) to the people of Arabia and beyond. Muhammad is therefore known as the Messenger as well as the Prophet. He called his people to believe in one God, and to follow God's guidance in leading a balanced and purposeful life, enabling the faithful to be rewarded with a place in paradise in the life after death. Muhammad wished himself and his followers to be a good example for the rest of society to follow – showing others how to abide by God's faith and rules.

The new faith: Islam

The Arabic word *Islam* means to surrender to the will of God, and obedience to his commands. The practices of the Muslim faith are widely varied among different communities all around the world. However, the five core 'pillars' of the faith are recognised by all. These are:

- The profession of faith (Shahadah);
- Daily prayers;
- Fasting during the month of Ramadan;
- Giving to the poor;
- Pilgrimage to the House of God in Makkah.

The Night of Destiny in Jerusalem, Palestine

A Muslim from Jerusalem explained that on this night families spend the whole night at the main mosques where sheikhs tell the story of Muhammad's vision. He described the night as follows:

'This is a night when one can be closest to God. It's better to say one prayer on Laylat-ul-Qadr than 1000 prayers at other times. Men go to the Al-Aqsa mosque, women to the As-Sakhrah mosque. The city's yards are also full of scouts and crowds.'

At this festival Muslims celebrate the change in worship from many statues to the One God, and thank God that He brought Islam. Before the occupation of Palestine, people used to come from all over the Muslim world for this day, with up to 250,000 visitors. Today there are fewer, perhaps 100,000 locals are permitted to travel. There used to be pilgrim hostels for travellers where they could lodge free on this day.

Shops stay open late into the night and doors are decorated with oil lamps.

The Night of Destiny in Turkey

A faithful Muslim from Turkey describes this as follows:

'After evening prayers, people move around the city from one mosque to another, praying in each till morning. There are stalls around each mosque selling food, and after each visit there is an opportunity to have a snack or a drink. In winter popular snacks are 'Sahlab' and chestnuts. In summer, rice with minced meat mixed in. Groups of friends will spend this night in this way even if they rarely go to the mosque at any other time.'

The Night of Destiny, a street in Jerusalem

Some mosques keep relics said to be hairs from the beard of the Prophet himself. On this night these relics are displayed in a glass case, which may be kissed in honour of the Prophet.

Prayers on this night are considered most auspicious and likely to be granted. While Laylat-ul-Qadr is normally celebrated on the 27th of the month of Ramadan, some consider that it may really fall on any of the odd-numbered days in the last 10 days of Ramadan (i.e. 21, 23, 25, 27 or 29). Some people pray through the night on all these days, to be sure to catch the real night.

Laylat-ul-Qadr in Iraq

It is believed that on this night the heavens open and God will receive and respond to every prayer and request from his worshippers. People stay up throughout the night to dawn, reading the Qur'an and praying. People will have started reading the Qur'an at the beginning of Ramadan, 26 days before this night, and endeavour to complete the reading on this special night.

'Patchah' an Iraqi lamb dish is cooked for this evening. Also, a sweet bread *'Churek'* and *'Halawat'* (halva) are made and sent to the mosques to be distributed among the poor, in remembrance of loved ones who have passed away.

Activity Ideas

+ Making an image of the Angel Gabriel to hang in the window

+ Making a rosary bead chain

+ Exploring Arabic writing

+ Making a bookmark with a name of God or prayer

+ Cooking Halawat Tahin (flour halva)

+ Making a book cover jacket

Activity 1: making an image of the Angel Gabriel to hang in the window

Materials:

Two sheets of white card (200g sheets)
Carbon paper
Stencil/cutting knife
Transparent plastic sheet (e.g. overhead projector sheets, etc.)
Colouring pens
Glitter (gold, silver, or any other colour)
Stained glass colours (or any other transparent colours)
Hole-puncher
Pencil
Glue or glue-stick
String or ribbon for hanging
One pin-board clip

Method:

1 Using the two cards, draw the image of the angel on both cards. You can use the carbon paper to trace the image onto the cards (by positioning the card *under* the page you wish to trace the pattern off. Then position the carbon paper between the pattern and the card, making sure that you put the carbon paper the right way up, with the black/blue plain side facing down onto the card).

2 Cut out the shaded parts of the silhouette using the stencil knife, making sure that you do not cut through the links that hold the whole silhouette together by mistake.

3 Colour the two angels. Make sure that you colour one looking to the left and one looking to the right, so that when positioning the transparent sheet between them, you have the angel coloured on both sides, back and front.

4 Draw the angel on the transparent plastic sheet.

5 Colour in the shaded parts, using the stained glass/transparent colours.

6 Use glitter if you like on both the card and the plastic sheet. You can apply the glue to the areas you want the glitter to go on and then sprinkle the glitter.

7 Leave all to dry.

8 When all the colouring is dry, glue the two frames and transparent sheet together.

9 Make a hole for hanging the silhouette, using the hole-puncher.

10 Attach the string or ribbon to the silhouette and hang against the window using the pin-board clip to fix to window frame.

Make an Image of Angel Gabriel to hang in the window

1) Make two tracings of the image above; one looking to the right, the other to the left

2) Cut out and discard the shaded parts, making sure not to cut through the links with the circle

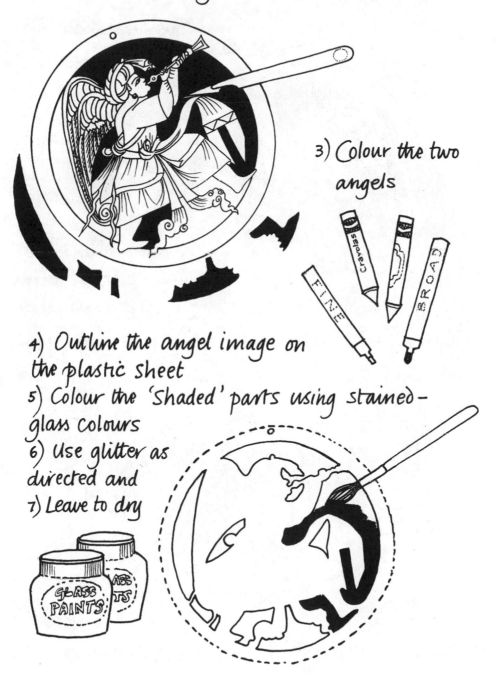

3) Colour the two angels

4) Outline the angel image on the plastic sheet
5) Colour the 'shaded' parts using stained-glass colours
6) Use glitter as directed and
7) Leave to dry

8) Glue front and back angel with transparent
sheet in the middle

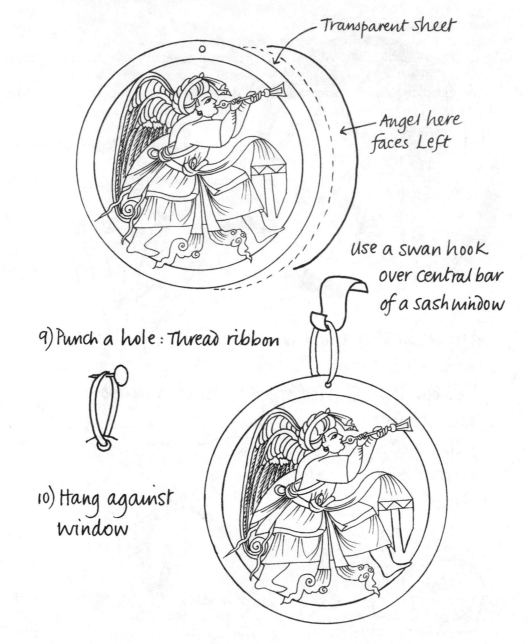

Transparent sheet

Angel here
faces Left

Use a swan hook
over central bar
of a sash window

9) Punch a hole : Thread ribbon

10) Hang against
window

Activity 2: making a rosary bead chain

The 'Misbahah or Subhah' rosary bead has been used by Muslims in religious recitations for many centuries. The Sufis adopted the use of the rosary bead from the Eastern Christians, who in turn adopted it from the Indian subcontinent traditions, and used it as a guide to devotions. The word 'Misbahah' means guidance in glorifying and praising God and his attributes (His names, see list below).

You can tell a Muslim rosary bead by the number of beads and sections in it. A full-length rosary bead has 99 beads (one for each of God's attributes/names). It is also common to find shorter rosary beads. These have a third of the full length, i.e. 33 beads. Each bead will then stand for three of God's names.

It is also fun to make the beads from modelling clay. This clay comes in several colours. Choose white, so that you are able to colour the beads. Air-hardening modelling material can be purchased from shops selling art materials and equipment. Roll the beads to the size you want, and make the holes before the clay hardens. Make sure that your holes are large, even if you are using a thin thread or string. *This is to enable you to use the rosary bead smoothly when praying and meditating.*

Materials:

Round and uniformly shaped and coloured beads (either 33 or 99 beads)

Flat disc-shaped beads, perhaps of a different colour, but should be of a similar diameter to the round beads (2 discs)

1 long or large oval-shaped bead, the bigger the better

Embroidery thread, thick, for making a tassel and threading the rosary. Choose a colour that complements the beads, and make sure that the thickness does not prevent threading the beads onto it.

Needle the right size for threading the beads

Scissors

Method:

1 Divide the beads into three equal quantities (11 or 33).
2 Prepare thread and needle. Make sure you have a long enough thread to allow for all the beads and a little bit extra. Don't knot the end of the thread.
3 Thread the first third of the beads.
4 Add one disc-shaped bead.
5 Thread the second third of the beads.
6 Add the second disc-shaped bead.
7 Thread the third lot of beads.
8 Join the two ends of the thread.
9 Thread the long bead and leave the chain of beads aside for the moment.
10 Make a tassel by cutting 12 equal lengths of thread (each 16cm long) and grouping them together.
11 Tie the chain of beads to the middle of the tassel's grouped threads.
12 Fold the tassel's threads and wrap with a piece of thread as in drawing.

Activity 3: exploring Arabic writing

As Arabic is written and read from right to left, letters and words are written starting with the top-right corner of a letter or word and ending with the bottom left-corner of it. Unlike English, Arabic can only be written with the individual letters joined up to create each word. The words, as in English, are lined up next to one another, with one empty space between, to make a row of text.

However, as the letters of a word are joined up, it is sometimes not necessary to leave a big gap, the size of a whole letter, between

words. This enables the calligrapher to fit many words into a small space. For this reason also, words can be written to overlap each other, partially or totally, creating highly stylised artistic texts.

We have written out some popular English names using the Arabic alphabet for you to practice writing. Remember to start at the top right corner working round to the bottom left. Some circular shapes need you to turn your hand round them.

Ann آن

Jessica جَسِّيكا

Becky بكي

Helena هَلنا

Victoria فكتوريا

Laura لورا

Joanne جَوان

Alice اليس

Chloë كلَوِي

Ashley اشلي

Zoë زَوَي

Caroline كارولين

Clare كلير

Sarah سارة

Gemma جَمّا

66

John جون

Peter پیتر

Ben بن

James جیمز

Tom توم

David دیڤید

Christopher کریستوفر

Oliver اولیڤر

Matthew ماثیو

Sam سام

Tim تیم

Neil نیل

Harry هاری

Lawrence لورَنس

Paul پول

Activity 4: making a bookmark with a name of God or prayer

You can use your name or that of a friend to make this bookmark. You may also wish to use one of the names of God for this activity.

Materials:
White or coloured card x 1 (190g)
Carbon paper x 1
Colouring pens or pencils
Pencil
Ruler
Scissors

Method:
1 Mark the borders of the bookmark on the card.
2 Design an appropriate border for your bookmark by using Islamic patterns (see sample patterns at back of book), or improvising your own. Make sure you leave enough space for the word you will copy onto the bookmark.
3 Using the carbon paper, trace the name of your choice onto the card (by positioning the card *under* the page you wish to trace the pattern off. Then position the carbon paper between the pattern and the card, making sure that you put the carbon paper the right way, with the black/blue plain side facing down onto the card).
4 Colour in the designs and calligraphy.
5 Cut out the bookmark.

(If desired, Islamic prayers may be copied onto the bookmark from the prayers in the next chapter, either in addition to one of the names of God, or instead.)

The 99 Names of God

These 99 names are revealed in the Qur'an as being attributes of God (see following pages).

GOD	ALLAH	ٱللَّٰه
1 The Abaser	Al-Khāfiḍ	ٱلْخَافِض
2 The Able	Al-Qādir	ٱلْقَادِر
3 The Alive	Al-Ḥayy	ٱلْحَي
4 The All-Embracing	Al-Wāsiʿ	ٱلْوَاسِع
5 The All-Forgiving	Al-Ghafūr	ٱلْغَفُور
6 The All-Hearing	As-Samūʿ	ٱلسَّمِيع
7 The All-Knowing	Al-ʿAlīm	ٱلْعَلِيم
8 The All-Relenting	At-Tawwāb	ٱلتَّوَّاب
9 The All-Seeing	Al-Baṣīr	ٱلْبَصِير
10 The Appreciative	Ash-Shakūr	ٱلشَّكُور

11 The Avenger	Al-Muntaqim	المُنْتَقِم
12 The Aware	Al-Khabīr	الخَبِير
13 The Beneficent	Ar-Rahmān	الرَّحْمٰن
14 The Bestower	Al-Wahhāb	الوَهَّاب
15 The Compassionate	Ar-Ra'uf	الرَّؤُوف
16 The Compeller	Al-Jabbār	الجَبَّار
17 The Constrictor	Al-Qābid	القَابِض
18 The Creator of Death	Al-Mumīt	المُمِيت
19 The Creator	Al-Khāliq	الخَالِق
20 The Delayer	Al-Mu'akhkhir	المُؤَخِّر
21 The Dishonourer	Al-Muzill	المُذِلّ
22 The Distresser	Ad-Dārr	الضَّار

23 The Enricher	Al-Mughnī	المُغْنِي
24 The Equitable	Al-Muqsiṭ	المُقْسِط
25 The Eternal Owner of Sovereignty	Mālik- ul-Mulk	مالِكِ الملك
26 The Eternal	Aṣ-Ṣamad	الصَّمَد
27 The Everlasting	Al-Bāqī	الباقِي
28 The Evolver	Al-Bāri'	البَارِئ
29 The Exalter	Ar-Rāfi'	الرَّافِع
30 The Expander	Al-Bāsiṭ	البَاسِط
31 The Expediter	Al-Muqaddim	المُقَدِّم
32 The Fashioner	Al-Muṣawwir	المُصَوِّر
33 The Finder	Al-Wājid	الوَاجِد
34 The Firm One	Al-Matīn	المَتِين

35 The First	Al-Awwal	الأَوَّلُ
36 The Forbearing One	Al-Ḥalīm	الْحَلِيمُ
37 The Forgiver	Al-Ghaffār	الْغَفَّارُ
38 The Gatherer	Al-Jāme'	الْجَامِعُ
39 The Generous One	Al-Karīm	الْكَرِيمُ
40 The Giver of Life	Al-Muḥyī	الْمُحْيِى
41 The Governor	Al-Wāli	الْوَالِى
42 The Great One	Al-'Azīm	الْعَظِيمُ
43 The Guardian of Faith	Al-Mu'min	الْمُؤْمِنُ
44 The Guide to the Right Path	Ar-Rashīd	الرَّشِيدُ
45 The Guide	Al-Hādī	الْهَادِى
46 The Hidden	Al-Bāṭin	الْبَاطِنُ

71

47 The Holy	Al-Quddūs	اَلْقُدُّوسُ
48 The Honourer	Al-Muʿizz	اَلْمُعِنُّ
49 The Incomparable	Al-Badīʿ	اَلْبَدِيعُ
50 The Judge	Al-Ḥakam	اَلْحَكَمُ
51 The Just	Al-ʿAdl	اَلْعَدْلُ
52 The Last	Al-Ākhir	اَلْآخِرُ
53 The Light	An-Nūr	اَلنُّورُ
54 The Lord of Majesty and Bounty	Dhul-Jalāl-Wal-Ikrām	ذُوالْجَلَالِ وَالْاِكْرَامِ
55 The Loving	Al-Wadūd	اَلْوَدُودُ
56 The Maintainer	Al-Muqīt	اَلْمُقِيتُ
57 The Majestic	Al-Mutakabbir	اَلْمُتَكَبِّرُ
58 The Manifest	Az-Ẓāhir	اَلظَّاهِرُ

72

59 The Mercy-Giving	Ar-Raḥīm	اَلرَّحِيم
60 The Mighty	Al-ʿAzīz	اَلعَزِيز
61 The Most Exalted	Al-Muta-ʿĀlī	المُتَعَالِي
62 The Most Glorious One	Al-Majīd	المَجِيد
63 The Most Great	Al-Kabīr	الكَبِير
64 The Most High	Al-ʿAlī	العَلِى
65 The Most Strong	Al-Qawī	القَوِى
66 The Noble	Al-Majīd	المَاجِد
67 The One	Al-Aḥad	الأَحَد
68 The Opener	Al-Fattāḥ	الفَتَّاح
69 The Originator	Al-Mubdī	المُبْدِى
70 The Pardoner	Al-ʿAfuw	العَفُو

73

71 The Patient	Aṣ-Ṣabūr	الصَّبُور
72 The Powerful	Al-Muqtadir	المُقْتَدِر
73 The Praiseworthy	Al-Ḥamīd	الحَمِيد
74 The Preserver	Al-Ḥafīz	الحَفِيظ
75 The Preventer	Al-Māni'	المَانِع
76 The Propitious	An-Nāfi'	النَّافِع
77 The Protecting Friend	Al-Walī	الوَلِي
78 The Protector	Al-Muhaymin	المُهَيْمِن
79 The Provider	Ar-Razzāq	الرَّزَّاق
80 The Reckoner	Al-Muhṣī	المُحْصِى
81 The Responsive	Al-Mujīb	المُجِيب
82 The Restorer	Al-Mu'īd	المُعِيد

83 The Resurrector	Al-Bā'ith	الْبَاعِث
84 The Self-Subsisting	Al-Qayyūm	الْقَيُّوم
85 The Self-Sufficient	Al-Ghanī	الْغَنِى
86 The Source of All Goodness	Al-Barr	الْبَرّ
87 The Source of Peace	As-Salām	أَلسَّلَام
88 The Sovereign Lord	Al-Malik	أَلْمَلِك
89 The Subduer	Al-Qahhār	الْقَهَّار
90 The Sublime One	Al-Jalīl	الْجَلِيل
91 The Subtle One	Al-Laṭīf	أَللَّطِيف
92 The Sufficient	Al-Ḥasīb	الْحَسِيب
93 The Supreme Inheritor	Al-Wārith	الْوَارِث
94 The Trustee	Al-Wakīl	الْوَكِيل

95 The Truth	Al-Ḥaqq	الْحَقُّ
96 The Unique	Al-Wāḥid	الْوَاحِدُ
97 The Watchful	Ar-Raqīb	الرَّقِيبُ
98 The Wise	Al-Ḥakīm	الْحَكِيمُ
99 The Witness	Ash-Shahīd	الشَّهِيدُ

Activity 5: cooking Halawat Tahin (flour halva)

This is a basic sweet dish, made with the simplest ingredients. This particular recipe is from Iraq. Its sweetness depends on taste, and can be adjusted by increasing the quantity of sugar used.

Ingredients:
1½ cups of white or brown plain flour
1½ - 2 cups of white sugar
2-3 cups of water
¾ cup vegetable oil
Almonds, peeled
Cardamom or rose water

Method:
1 Dissolve the sugar in the water. You can boil it on the stove for five minutes to help the process; then add the cardamom.

76

2 On medium heat, in a separate pan, heat the oil and fry the almonds in it, removing them quickly as they turn to a light golden colour. (If the almonds or oil darken or burn, discard them, or otherwise you will have a burnt flavour in the sweet).

3 Keeping the remainder of the oil in the pan on the stove, add the flour to it, and mix in well, until the flour becomes golden in colour.

4 Remove from the stove and add the dissolved sugar syrup and half the almonds, mixing them well together.

5 Return the mixture to a reduced heat, stirring it continuously until it forms into a thick lump that does not stick to the sides of the pan. If you find the mixture is too soft, continue to heat and mix until it thickens. If the opposite is the case, add a little boiled water while still mixing.

6 Serve in a dish, decorating with the remaining half of the fried almonds.

Optional: you can substitute milk for half of the water. You can add 2 tablespoons of cocoa, mixing it in at the last stage (5).

Activity 6: making a book cover jacket

Wherever it was practised Islam encouraged the seeking of knowledge. The art of book binding, page gilding, and miniature painting flourished in Muslim countries. The Qur'an, as well as many other scientific and literary books, was highly decorated and illustrated. Why not design your own book cover? You can choose a book that is special to you, a personal diary for example.

For the purposes of this activity, we have chosen a standard sized 'Letts 32X' weekly appointments diary (21.5cm x 14.5cm).

Materials:

Felt sheets, several colours. You will need one large sheet that will be cut to make the actual jacket for the book (approximately 60cm x 30cm)

Coloured thread appropriate for sewing felt

Needle, an appropriate size for the felt

Sewing pins

Glue, suitable for felt

Tracing paper

Carbon paper

Scissors

Method:

1 Plan the design you want, and work out the measurements of the jacket (including the inside flaps).

2 Mark out the jacket and the flaps.

3 Choose from the patterns suggested and trace them out.

4 Choose one of the felt colours and cut out the full jacket. Make sure that you allow extra felt round all the edges for folding and sewing together.

5 Choose the different parts of the cover design from the other felt colours, and cut the shapes out.

6 Stitch the design pieces on to the background felt piece. If you choose to glue as opposed to sewing the designs, make sure that you at least stitch the corners down (take care in using the glue, as too much glue may stain the felt pieces).

7 You may wish to use several layers to make up your design. This will give a three-dimensional effect which would look very nice if you are using several shades of a colour.

8 When you have finished the felt cover stitch the edges and the flaps to complete the book cover jacket.

9 Dress up the diary/book in your new jacket.

Make a Book Jacket

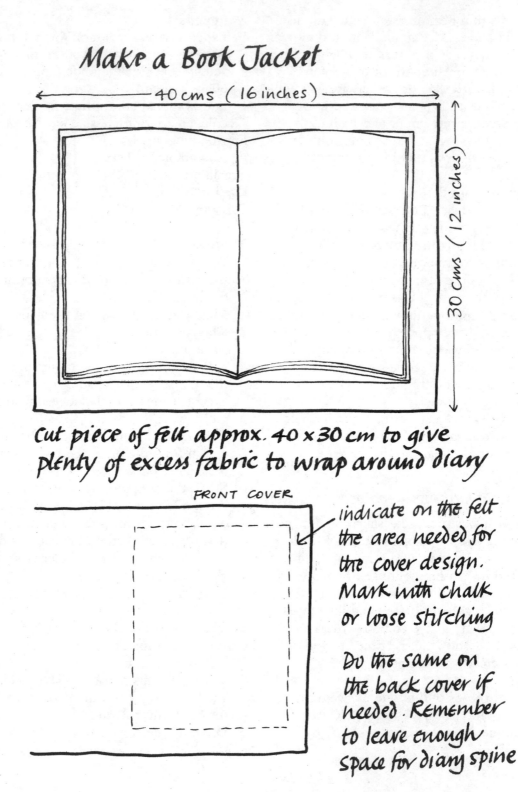

40 cms (16 inches)

30 cms (12 inches)

Cut piece of felt approx. 40 x 30 cm to give plenty of excess fabric to wrap around diary

FRONT COVER

indicate on the felt the area needed for the cover design. Mark with chalk or loose stitching

Do the same on the back cover if needed. Remember to leave enough space for diary spine

Choose a simple pattern from the designs at the back of this book or you could simplify one section of a more complex design———

Trace the pattern onto the felt and cut out the various components in felts of different colours

Assemble the pattern. Pin down the pieces. Use small running stitches or an overlapping stitch
- - - - or ///// taking out the pins as you go

Embroider your design!

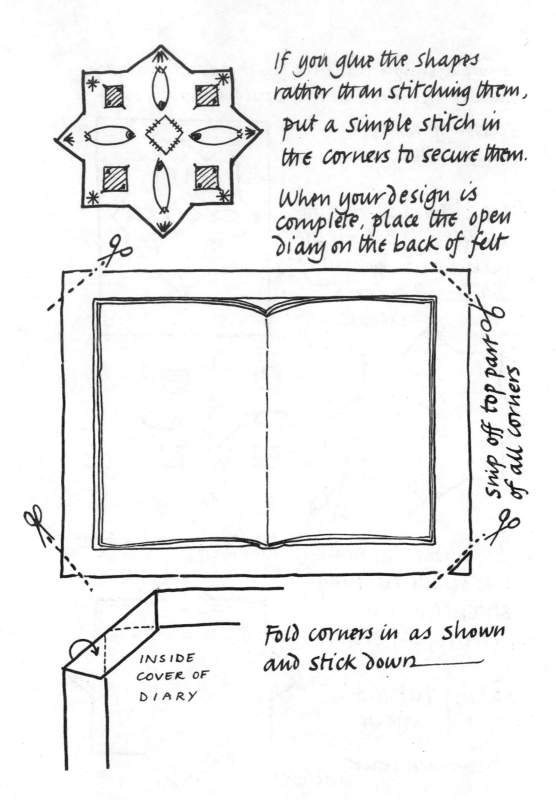

If you glue the shapes rather than stitching them, put a simple stitch in the corners to secure them.

When your design is complete, place the open diary on the back of felt

snip off top part of all corners

Fold corners in as shown and stick down

INSIDE COVER OF DIARY

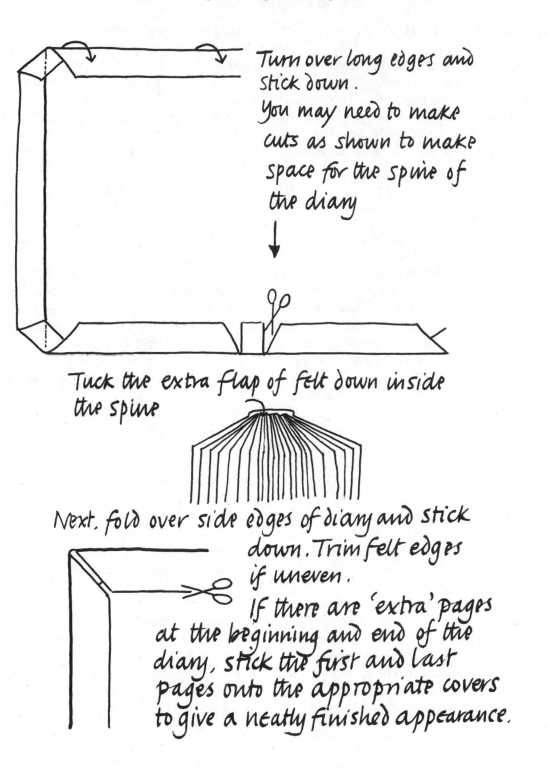

Turn over long edges and stick down.
You may need to make cuts as shown to make space for the spine of the diary

Tuck the extra flap of felt down inside the spine

Next, fold over side edges of diary and stick down. Trim felt edges if uneven.
If there are 'extra' pages at the beginning and end of the diary, stick the first and last pages onto the appropriate covers to give a neatly finished appearance.

Stories about Faith

The first pillar of Islam affirms belief in a single God, and the message which Muhammad brought from God. This faith in God and God's will on earth is at the heart of Islam, and is echoed in folktales throughout the Muslim world which affirm the importance of faith.

The Angel of Death

This story was written by a Muslim poet called Jalalladin Rumi. Rumi was born in the town of Balkh, in what is now Afghanistan, at the beginning of the 13th Century. He was born at a time when Mogul warriors were building a great empire. Rumi and his family fled from the invading army and travelled west, living in many places and completing the pilgrimage to Makkah, before Rumi finally settled in the town of Konya in what is now western Turkey.

His religious poetry is famous throughout the world. He was the leader of a group of holy men, or Sufis, who sought to know God through meditation and prayer. Sufi, literally, means one who wears wool. They were called Sufis because they wore simple, rough clothes made from wool, shunning expensive clothes and outward appearance.

Many Sufi masters have taught their disciples by asking them to contemplate stories, providing a wealth of folktales, fables and wonder tales which are enjoyed today by Muslims and non-Muslims alike. Many of the stories involve prophets from the Christian and Jewish faiths, who are also recognised as prophets in Islam.

Once the great King Solomon was sitting in his palace in Jerusalem, when a man rushed into the room, flustered and out of breath. His face was pale and he was clearly terrified.

'Speak Man! Tell me what bothers you!' commanded King Solomon.

'Your majesty, I have just seen the Angel of Death. I was walking in the street when he came up to me, stared at me long and hard, and then disappeared. I'm sure he plans to come back and take my life!'

'My dear man,' replied Solomon, 'the Angel of Death takes all his orders from God. He only does as God commands. So he won't do anything to you until God gives the order. There's no need to be afraid – seeing the Angel doesn't mean that you will die.'

'But I *am* afraid,' protested the man. I have always been afraid of death, and now I've seen the Angel's angry look, I am even more afraid. Your majesty, people say that the winds obey you. Please ask the wind to send me away from here, to another land, far away from the Angel of Death. Please, they say you help the needy, so please …help me! Send me to India far away from death!'

Solomon had pity on the man. He let him sit on his flying carpet, and asked the wind to take him wherever he asked. The man asked to go to a particular city in India, and the winds blew him there.

The next day, Solomon happened to meet the Angel of Death, and asked him about the man.

'Yesterday, a man came to my palace frightened because he saw you staring at him in the street. He asked to get as far away from here as he could, so I sent him off to India. I'm curious though. Tell me – why did you frighten him so much he had to leave his home and live in a foreign land?'

The Angel of Death gave Solomon a strange look:

'Solomon, you know that I never do anything without the express orders of God. I didn't mean to scare the man. It was just

that yesterday, when I saw him in Jerusalem, I looked at him with surprise and astonishment. God had told me to go to India later in the day and there take the soul of that same man. I thought to myself 'How can he get there? How could he reach India by the afternoon? Even a bird could not fly there fast enough. Since it was not yet time for his death, I passed him by and then, at the proper time I went to India and there he was, just as God had said. So I took him, and he died.'

Solomon nodded:

'Death is destiny – it is certain that none can escape it. He asked to go to India to escape death, and in doing so went to meet the thing he sought to avoid.'

Trust in God

While trusting in God's will is basic to Islam, that does not mean Muslims should wait for the inevitable to happen. It is said that once the Prophet was asked why people should tie their camels up when they came to the mosque. Surely, if they wandered away, that would be the will of God?

Muhammad replied with the now famous proverb:

'Trust in God, but tether your camel'

This story, from Iran, affirms the importance of faith, and the benefits it may bring.

Once there were three friends, Vafai, Sanai, and Allahi. One year they decided to travel to a distant land in search of work. They travelled to the place, worked for a year and then began their journey home with the money they had saved. On the way they came to the city of Bazardan, where a great king lived.

They were looking around for a place to stay the night when they came to the palace gardens and decided to spend the night in a sheltered corner of the garden. As it grew dark the air became chilly, so the men collected twigs and branches and built a small fire to keep them warm.

It happened that there was a shortage of trees in the kingdom. In order to save wood the king had given orders that no one in the city was to light fires. When he looked out of his window that night he saw the flames of the fire and decided to go and see who was disobeying his order.

He crept up to the three men, and hid behind a tree, and listened to their conversation. They were chatting about what they would ask for if the king gave them a wish.

'The king must be a very rich man,' said Vafai. 'If the king gave me a bag of his gold, then I could go home a rich man.'

Sanai shook his head:

'Gold is all very well,' he said, 'but if the king let me marry his daughter, then I would really be happy and comfortable. That would be my wish from him.'

Allahi disagreed with his two friends.

'I don't want anything from the king, however rich he is,' said Allahi. 'He may be rich, but that doesn't impress me at all! All I want is what God chooses to give me. Nothing more!'

The king listened a while longer and then returned to the palace, thinking that he would teach Allahi a lesson for not showing him proper respect. The next day he brought the three friends to his chambers. He ordered them to repeat what they had wished for last night. When Vafai asked for gold, the king presented him with a large sack of gold. When Sanai asked to marry a princess, the king gave his youngest daughter. When Allahi repeated his wish for nothing, the king shouted at him:

'Fine, then leave with nothing! Away with you now!'

The king expected Allahi to beg for a gift, but Allahi just smiled and respectfully thanked him. The three men bowed and walked away from the king's chambers, Vafai carrying his sack of gold and Sanai walking hand in hand with his new bride, the princess.

'Let God take care of you then!' shouted the king as the three friends left.

The King sat in his palace fuming, and after a few hours he decided that Allahi should be punished for this disrespect, and he summoned one of his soldiers.

'Follow those three men,' he said, 'and kill the one without either the gold or my daughter.'

The soldier saluted, saddled up his horse, and rode off in pursuit.

The three friends and the princess walked all day down the road to their village, but after a few hours Vafai grew tired.

'It's too heavy,' he protested.

Allahi kindly offered to help, and carried the sack for a while. It happened that, while Allahi was carrying the sack, the soldier sent by the king caught up with the men. He galloped straight at Vafai, and with sword drawn, chopped off his head. He then wheeled his horse around and returned to the palace, reporting to the king that his mission was completed.

Sanai and Allahi were saddened, frightened and puzzled by the death of their friend. They buried him in a grave by the roadside and continued along the road towards home.

A while later they came to a strong deep river. Sanai tried to carry the princess across the river but half way across he lost his footing, and he and the princess were swept away. Allahi jumped in to rescue them, but was only able to save the princess. His friend could not swim, and drowned in the raging river.

Sad and distressed, Allahi and the princess continued their journey, taking with them the bag of gold. Around nightfall they reached an inn with an empty cottage next to it. After they had eaten supper, they asked the innkeeper if they could stay the night in the cottage.

'Don't stay there!' warned the innkeeper. 'Everyone who stays the night in the cottage is found dead in the morning. It's better for you to go to the village and stay there somewhere!'

But Allahi and the princess said they were not afraid of superstition, and they would be happy to spend the night in the cottage. The innkeeper reluctantly agreed and unlocked the cottage for the travellers.

Once inside, Allahi was so tired that he fell asleep almost immediately.

The princess stayed awake, keeping guard in case anything happened in the night. In her pocket she had an enchanted knife that her grandmother had given her for protection. Sensing danger, she took the knife from her pocket and waited.

Around midnight she saw a stone slab moving in front of her on the ground. As it opened she saw there was a tunnel under the slab going deep into the ground. When a horrible monster started crawling up out of the tunnel she rushed at it and struck it with her knife, cutting off half its head. The creature gave a terrible scream, then looked up at the princess and said:

'Kill me! Please kill me now! I will only die slowly and painfully if you do not. Look, down below there are caves full of treasure I have taken from travellers. Kill me quickly and it can all be yours.'

The princess did as she was asked, chopping the creature's head clean off. Then she woke up Allahi, and told him what had happened. Together they explored the caves under the cottage. There were forty caves in all, each one crammed full of treasure.

The next morning the innkeeper was surprised to see the couple still alive, and even more surprised when they said they liked it so much they wanted to buy the cottage. He readily agreed, and soon the cottage was theirs. The innkeeper was so keen to get away from the haunted cottage that he sold them the inn too, and went to a new tavern in another village.

Allahi and the princess took over the tavern, and with their new wealth they rebuilt and improved the inn till it was

famous throughout the land for its fine rooms and delicious food.

Years later, the king and queen were on a journey and stopped to stay at the tavern for the night. Allahi received the king, but the king did not recognise him.

'Your majesties,' he said. 'Please let me show you around my inn. I have 40 fine rooms, and I am willing to show you 39 of them.'

The King and Queen were amazed at the treasures which filled every room. When the tour was finished they asked why they had not been shown the last room in the house.

'It is not permitted!' said Allahi, simply.

That night, the queen was so curious that she couldn't sleep. She slipped out of her bedroom and went to the fortieth room. When she opened the door, Allahi and the princess were inside.

'This is my wife,' he said.

The queen was overjoyed to recognise her daughter and asked what had happened since she had left. The princess told the whole story.

'So you see Mother,' she concluded. 'All this treasure belongs to us. The poor man who wanted nothing from a king, and trusted in God, is now rich and my husband!' When the king heard the story he realised that trust in God is the best path to true happiness. Allahi and the princess moved to the palace, and when the King died Allahi ruled justly and wisely in his place.

The King and the Baker

This story was collected in Iraq, although tales like it are found all over the Muslim world. Like the Juha story in the last chapter, insh'allah, meaning 'God willing' features prominently in the tale.

Once there was a king who liked to walk around the streets of his city in disguise, so that no one would recognise him, and see how his subjects lived. One evening he was walking the streets dressed in the clothes of a foreigner when he heard the sound of singing. It was coming from a baker's shop. The king looked in at the door and saw the baker weighing out flour to make loaves of bread. As he worked he chanted:

'Insh'allah, insh'allah, insh'allah for me
If that's as God wills it, then so let it be!'

The king was unsure whether the baker really meant what he said. Such a public display of faith might just be for show: he decided to put the baker's faith to the test.

The king walked into the shop and addressed the baker:

'Excuse me sir: I need a loaf of bread but have come out with no money. Give me some bread and I'll leave this ring. It's very valuable. I'll come back tomorrow, pick up the ring and pay for the bread at the same time.'

'Certainly,' said the baker. 'Whatever God wills, so be it!'

So the king took away a loaf of bread, and the baker put the expensive ring in his cash box.

The next day the king ordered his adviser to get the ring back from the baker without him knowing. The adviser went to the baker's shop and told the baker he had come to check all the weights he used. While the baker was busy bringing weights, the adviser opened his cash box, took out the ring and put it in his pocket. In this way the king soon had his ring back.

The next day the baker was summoned to appear before the king.

'My good fellow,' said the king. 'Yesterday I came into your shop, left my ring there and took away some bread. I didn't tell you I was the king but now you know. The ring is worth a small fortune. Give it to me and I will pay for the bread.'

'Your majesty,' replied the baker, 'The ring has gone. I'm afraid I don't know where it is!'

'What!' roared the king. 'Disappeared? My priceless ring! You must return it within ten days, or you will pay with your life!'

The next day the baker presented the ring to the king. The latter examined it, amazed that it was indeed the ring that he had asked the baker to find. He had given the man an impossible task, and God had intervened to save him.

The king patted the baker on the shoulder.

'God has taken care of you, my pious friend.'

The king rewarded the baker with a great box filled with gold, silver and jewels, and from that day on the king himself started saying:

'Insh'allah, insh'allah, insh'allah for me
If that's as God wills it, then so let it be!'

The baker returned home, worried and confused, but kept repeating to himself :

'Insh'allah, insh'allah, insh'allah for me
If that's as God wills it, then so let it be!'

After nine days of waiting, the baker decided to go fishing, and enjoy the last day before his death. It happened that on the same day the king went hunting in the forest where the baker was fishing. The king stopped by the river to wash his hands, and while he was washing the ring slipped from his fingers and was swept away in the current.

A while later, the baker caught a large fat salmon and took it home for his wife to cook.

'This is our last happy meal together!' he said to his wife.

When she cut the fish open to take out the bone, she found a gold ring in the stomach. She showed it to her husband and he recognised it as the king's ring.

Chapter 4

A MIRACULOUS JOURNEY

Glory to God Who did take his servant for a journey by night, from the Sacred Mosque [the Ka'bah in Makkah] to the Farthest Mosque [the Dome of the Rock in Jerusalem] whose precincts we did bless, in order that we might show him some of our signs. For God is the One Who hears and sees all.

The Qur'an: *Surat Al-Isra*

The Night Journey

In previous chapters we read how Muhammad was born and raised in the holy city of Makkah, into a family responsible for taking care of the sacred Ka'bah, or House of God. At the age of forty he began his work as a prophet, after the Angel Gabriel visited him and began to reveal to him the words of the Qur'an.

Exile in Makkah

Year by year, as the number of people following Muhammad's teaching grew, so did opposition to his new message from the tribal chiefs of Makkah. Muhammad's followers were ridiculed, attacked and sometimes killed for their beliefs, and many left for other towns where they would not be persecuted.

Things got worse and worse for the Muslims, until one day an order calling for a boycott of Muhammad's clan (the 'Bani Hashim') was nailed to the wall of the House of God. It stated that there should be no trade or marriage between the other tribes of Makkah and Muhammad's tribe. (Such a boycott would lead to extreme poverty for his clan, as many were traders and merchants.)

When Muhammad and his followers saw the order, they decided to move to a rocky hillside on the outskirts of the town, where they lived in terrible poverty. The chiefs tried to prevent food or water being brought to them, leading to much suffering for Muhammad and his followers. Some food was smuggled in at night, but conditions were harsh, and hunger and disease were common.

Muhammad's tribe had been living like this for three years, when some of Makkah's tribal chiefs began to question whether the boycott should continue. They saw the suffering of the Bani Hashim, which included some of their own relatives. One leader, Zuhair, went to the House of God, and called out to the worshippers there:

'People of Makkah! We eat good food and dress in good clothes while the Bani Hashim are dying because no one will trade with them. In God's name I vow that I will not rest until the unjust order has been torn up!'

One of Zuhair's supporters went into the House of God to tear up the boycott order, but inside they saw that the piece of paper had been eaten by insects, except for the top of the paper where the words 'In your name, O God,' could still be read.'

This was taken as a sign from God that the boycott should cease, and Muhammad's tribe returned to their homes inside Makkah.

The Night Journey

Muhammad had been teaching for ten years when his uncle died. Abu Taleb had cared for him since childhood, and Muhammad grieved at his death. Soon after this, his beloved wife Khadijeh died, adding a second deep sadness to the first.

Soon after her death, the Angel Gabriel appeared to Muhammad at night. He led Muhammad outside to a white mule with wings attached to its thighs. This was the buraq, the spirit horse which had carried previous prophets including Abraham himself. Muhammad mounted the buraq, which immediately flew high into the air. Escorted by Gabriel, they flew over many lands until they arrived in Jerusalem. Waiting for them there were Abraham, Moses, Jesus and many other prophets. Muhammad was asked to lead them in prayer, and he did so.

After the prayers three dishes were placed in front of Muhammad, and he was asked to choose one. One contained water, one wine and the third milk. Muhammad told the prophets that he had once heard a prophecy that if he chose water the community of Muslims would drown; if he chose wine then they would be led astray from the good life; but if he chose milk then Muhammad and the Muslim community would be guided along the right path of the true religion. Accordingly the Prophet chose the dish of milk and drank from it. Gabriel then told Muhammad that he and his followers would be guided to the true religion of one God.

From Jerusalem, Muhammad travelled up into the sky until he reached the first gate of heaven. The gate was guarded by an angel, Ishmael, who had 12,000 angels under his command. Each of those angels was in charge of another 12,000 angels, all of them guarding the gate.

As Gabriel led Muhammad through the gate, Ishmael asked who was with him. When Gabriel answered that Muhammad was with him, Ishmael asked, 'Is this the one who has been sent to deliver God's message to man?' When Gabriel said it was, Ishmael said some prayers for Muhammad and let him pass.

Muhammad climbed through seven heavenly worlds, where he met many of the ancient prophets once again, including Jesus, John the Baptist, Jacob (son of Joseph), Moses and Abraham. He then passed through a second gate, again guarded by thousands of angels, into paradise. There he met and spoke with God, who explained to him the importance of regular prayer for all believers.

On his way back from paradise, Muhammad met Moses, who asked him how many prayers God had ordered for his followers.

'Fifty a day,' replied Muhammad.

'That's too many,' said Moses, 'Go back to God and ask to have them reduced.'

Muhammad did as Moses suggested and God agreed the number should be reduced to 10 prayers a day, but when Muhammad returned, Moses said that ten was still too much and he should get a further reduction.

This time God agreed that Muslims should pray only five times a day. Moses thought this still too many, but Muhammad refused to go back to God again, saying he would be embarrassed to do so. The Prophet continued on his journey and returned that night to Makkah.

After his return to Makkah, Muhammad described to his followers the journey he had made and the new instruction concerning prayer five times a day. This teaching was to become the second main teaching (or pillar) of Islam.

At first, many of his followers did not believe his story. 'How could Muhammad travel to Jerusalem in one night, when the trade caravan took a month to get there and another month to get back?' they wondered.

Some stopped believing in the Prophet because of this story, while others went to a close friend of the prophet, Abu Bakr, and told him what had happened. Abu Bakr went to Muhammad and asked him to describe, in detail, what he had seen in Jerusalem. When he had finished, Abu Bakr, who had been to Jerusalem, declared that all the details were accurate and that the Prophet must be speaking the truth.

However, as Muhammad won more and more converts to Islam, there was growing opposition to him from tribes within Makkah.

The Significance of the Journey

In Arabic this event is known as *Al-Isra wa Al-Miraj,* meaning 'the Night Journey' and ascension. This marks an event which is said to have occurred on the night of the 24th Rajab 619AD (see Chapter 5 for explanation of Muslim calendar).

The first part of the journey was a flight across the Arabian desert from Makkah to Jerusalem at night.

The second part of the journey was from Jerusalem upwards through the seven heavens, to the throne of God. Muhammad made this journey with the Archangel Gabriel, riding on the back of a white mule, the *buraq.*

Islam is one of the three main monotheistic religions, the others being Christianity and Judaism. It recognises all the prophets in the Bible. On his journey Muhammad received the blessing and advice of several such prophets including Moses and Jesus.

The journey had an important role in shaping the worship practices of the Muslim faith, as well as several lessons of spiritual value to the Prophet and his followers. This journey also confirms to Muslims God's promise of the coming of Judgement Day, and the existence of heaven for those who lead good lives, and hell for those who deliberately disobey God's will.

Celebrating the Night Journey in Jerusalem

On the night of *Al-Isra wa Al-Miraj,* a special Jerusalem sweet bread called *'Mshabbak'* is made and sold by street vendors. The story of the ascension of the Prophet is told in the mosques. Prayers are said throughout the day, which is a public holiday. As everyone stays up all night, the shops stay open until late in the evening. All the doors of the houses are decorated with lamps, and most people will head for the main mosque for evening prayers and celebrations.

What did Abraham, Moses, and Jesus look like?

The Prophet Muhammad is said to have described these prophets as follows:

'As for Abraham, I have not seen anyone who looked like him, but I have not seen anyone who did not look like him either. As for Moses, he was tall, tanned, and slim, had curly hair, and had a hooked nose. As for Jesus, he is red-skinned, neither tall nor short, with straight hair, and many moles on his face. He seemed to have just come out of a bath. His hair seemed to be wet though it was not.'

What did Muhammad see in each of the seven heavens?

The Prophet Muhammad described what he saw in each of the seven heavens:

'When I entered the World's Sky (the first heaven), I saw a man sitting there who was being shown the souls of humans. When he saw a good soul he would smile and say,

"A pleasant soul from a pleasant body."

When he saw wicked souls he would frown and say,

"A wicked soul from a wicked body."

I asked Gabriel: "Who is this person?" He replied: "This is your father Adam, who is being shown the souls of his descendants."

Then Gabriel elevated me to the Second Sky. There I saw Jesus, son of Mary, and John, son of Zachariah (see Chapter 1).

Then Gabriel elevated me to the Third Sky. There I saw a man who had a face as handsome as the face of the full moon (Al-Badr).

I asked, "Who is this man, O Gabriel?"

He replied, "This is your brother, Joseph, the son of Jacob."

Then Gabriel elevated me to the Fourth Sky. There I saw a man. I asked Gabriel who he was. He told me he was the prophet Idris (an Old Testament prophet, from before the flood).

Then Gabriel elevated me to the Fifth Sky, where I saw an old man with a white head and a great white beard. I had not seen a more handsome old man than him. I said: "Who is this man, O Gabriel?" He said: "This is Harun (Moses' older brother), the beloved one amongst his people."

Then he elevated me to the Sixth Sky, where there was a tall man with a hooked nose, who looked like a man from the Shnou'e tribe. I asked Gabriel: "Who is this man?" He said: "This is your brother Moses, the son of Imran."

Then he elevated me to the Seventh Sky where I saw an old man sitting on a chair by the gate to paradise, where 70,000 angels pass through every day, and do not come out again until Judgement Day. I have not seen anyone who looked like him, but I have not seen anyone who did not look like him either. I asked Gabriel: "Who is this man?" He said: "This is your father Abraham." Then Gabriel took me into paradise.'

The importance of prayer and worship

Guard strictly your prayers. Especially the middle prayer; and stand before God devotedly.
          The Qur'an: *Surat Al-Baqarah*

After the Night Journey, as we saw, Muhammad instructed his followers to pray five times a day. Muslims believe that through prayer we may all communicate with God. During prayer a Muslim will thank God for all the blessings and help given to him.

According to the Qur'an, 'Prayer may be spoken or silent. It may include praise, confession, thanksgiving, repentance and meditation on behalf of oneself or another person.'

The five daily prayers are conducted at fixed times of day and in specific ways. They take place at dawn, noon, afternoon, dusk, and night. They are usually conducted alone, in private or at the mosque, but are sometimes carried out together in large groups, especially at the Friday noon prayer.

All five daily prayers involve standing, sitting and bowing according to an exact pattern. Each cycle of standing, sitting and bowing is

known as a prostration or Raka'h. At the dawn prayer, worshippers complete two prostrations; at noon, afternoon and night prayers four prostrations are required; and at sunset three are made.

No matter what a Muslim person's language is, the five daily prayers are made in classical Arabic (the original language of the Qur'an), and are uttered to oneself and not spoken aloud. The eyes are kept open, looking straight ahead. Men and women say the prayers in exactly the same way. They do not take long to perform, the longest taking no more than 10 – 15 minutes.

The daily prayer

1 Standing up, the worshipper declares that he intends to pray to God the prayer for that time of day.
2 Then he/she acknowledges that God is great: *(Allah-u-Akbar)*.
3 Then God is praised and thanked for his Majesty and sought as shelter from Satan. The 'Fatiha', Chapter 1 of the Qur'an, is recited (see following page), and another short chapter.
4 Next the worshipper bows and declares 'God is mighty' three times.
5 The worshipper stands again and recites a verse acknowledging that God listens to those who praise Him.

6 Then the worshipper kneels down and touches the ground with the forehead, declaring that 'God is the Highest' three times.

7 Sitting upright, he/she acknowledges that God is great.

8 The genuflecting (touching the ground with forehead) is repeated a second time saying 'God is the highest' three times.

9 Then he/she stands up, and this marks the end of the first prostration. The second prostration starts with God being declared great, then the 'Fatiha' is recited and a second short chapter from the Qur'an.

10 Steps 4-9 are repeated as many times as is required.

11 On completing the required number of prostrations, the worshipper, in the seated position, recites verses stating that 'there is no god but God and Muhammad is his Messenger'. Finally there is a request to God to bestow his blessing upon the Prophet and his descendants, the good worshippers, and Abraham and his descendants.

12 The worshipper then turns to the right saying: Peace be upon you and thanks be to God for his blessings. This is repeated to the left. The prayer is then complete.

Prayers from the Qur'an

In the name of God the Compassionate, the Merciful. Praise be to God, Lord of the Universe, the Compassionate, the Merciful, Sovereign of the Day of judgement! You alone we worship, and to You alone we turn for help. Guide us to the straight path, the path of those whom You have favoured, not of those who have incurred Your wrath, nor of those who have gone astray.

Surat Al-Fatiha

Say: truly, my prayer and my service of sacrifice, my life and my death, are all for God, the Cherisher of the Worlds, no partners has he. This am I commanded, and I am the first of those who bow to His will.

(Chapter 6, verses 162-163)

Our Lord, give us good in this life and good in the hereafter, and protect us from the torment of the hell fire.   (Chapter 2, verse 201)

O my Lord, bestow wisdom on me, and join me with the righteous.

(Chapter 26, verse 83)

Moses prayed to God: 'O my Lord, relieve my bosom of its concerns, ease the task at my hand, and remove the impediment from my speech, so that others may understand what I say.'

(Chapter 20, verses 25-28)

Abraham said to God: 'Our Lord, make us submissive to You, and of our descendants a people submissive to You; and show us our religious rites, and forgive us, for You are the Forgiver, the Merciful.'

(Chapter 2, verse 128)

Other well-known prayers

The Prophet Muhammad said: 'In Your Name, O Lord, I lay my side to sleep, and by Your leave I raise it up. If You take away my soul during sleep, forgive it; and if You send it back, protect it as You protect Your pious servants.[1]

O God, make me content with Your judgement, make me patient in the face of Your tribulation, and imbue me with gratitude for Your blessings. I beg You to grant the perfection of Your blessing, the permanence of Your gift of well-being, and the maintenance of Your love.[2]

O God, let us be among those who see you in this world with the eyes of the heart, and in the hereafter with the eyes of the head.[3]

O God, enliven the bodies of our deeds with the spirit of sincere devotion to you.[4]

O God, if I worship You in fear of hell, burn me in it. If I worship You in hope of paradise, exclude me from it. But if I worship You for Your own sake, do not deny me Your ever-lasting beauty.[5]

Why do Muslims use a prayer rug?

It is not compulsory for Muslims to use a prayer rug, but it is a common tradition in many countries. It helps ensure the floor space one is praying on is clean.

Most rugs are woven little carpets with a pile, but some are made from felt (matted wool) and are embroidered with coloured woollen thread by hand. Often rugs have images of the Ka'bah and the Prophet's mosque in Madinah on the upper side of the rug. However, there are several other styles that may include decorated arches, elaborate oil lamps or flowers.

The average size of a modern prayer rug is 65cm x 110cm. The rug is normally kept folded in a clean place, and is spread out at times of prayer facing towards Makkah (in Britain, this would be towards the South East), with the top edge of the rug in that direction. Some prayer rugs are used as decorative wall-hangings in the home.

In Uganda, prayer mats are woven from the leaves of a particular tree, the insahsah. Women and children collect the leaves, and then boil them up with dyes to make particular colours, before weaving the long thin strips together.

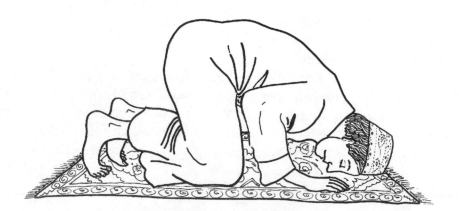

The call to prayer

English translation		Arabic
God is great	(said four times)	Allah-u-Akbar
I bear witness that there is no god but God	(said twice)	Ashhadu 'an la 'ilaha 'illa-Allah
I bear witness that Muhammad is God's Messenger	(said twice)	Ashhadu 'an Muhammadan Rasul-Allah
Come to prayer	(said twice)	Hayyi 'ala-il-salah
Come to success	(said twice)	Hayyi 'ala-il-fala'
God is great, God is great There is no god but God		Allah-u-Akbar, Allah-u-Akbar 'ilaha 'illa-Allah

The call to prayer

The call to prayer is made from the mosque's minaret (tower). The caller alerts the people of the neighbourhood that it is time to pray, by reciting a specific set of verses. These are recited in Arabic in all countries, whatever the native language (see above).

Activity Ideas

✦ Making a Seven Heavens mobile

✦ Making a prayer rug

✦ Making a collage/mosaic of the Dome of the Rock, Jerusalem

✦ Cooking Halawat Al-Jizer (carrot halva)

Activity 1: making a Seven Heavens mobile

Materials:
Card, white and coloured
Colouring pencils, pens, paints
Glitter and metallic colours
Glue
Fishing line (nylon wire) or strong
    thread
Scissors
Hole punch or big needle
Craft/stencil knife
Tracing/carbon paper
Ballpoint pen or pencil

Method:
1 Make 2 copies onto card of the individual parts of the mobile. The struts should be on white card as they represent clouds.

2 Cut carefully around each shape as indicated in the drawings.

3 Colour each part – add glitter if desired.

4 Stick each pair together with designs facing outward.

5 Pierce holes for hanging where indicated on each image.

6 In a metre-length of space, arrange the separate parts of the mobile in position according to the diagram.

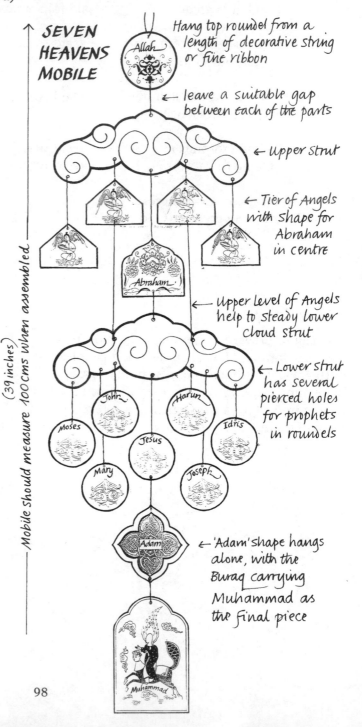

SEVEN HEAVENS MOBILE

Hang top roundel from a length of decorative string or fine ribbon

← leave a suitable gap between each of the parts

← Upper strut

← Tier of Angels with shape for Abraham in centre

← Upper level of Angels help to steady lower cloud strut

← Lower strut has several pierced holes for prophets in roundels

← 'Adam' shape hangs alone, with the Buraq carrying Muhammad as the final piece

Mobile should measure 100 cms when assembled (39 inches)

Upper Strut of Seven Heavens Mobile:

Copy and cut out
2 of these cloud
struts. Stick back to
back and pierce holes as
indicated to hang from top
roundel and to dangle the
angel and Abraham shapes

❀ Upper parts of the Seven Heavens Mobile:

← Copy 2 of these roundels and stick them back to back

Make holes top & bottom where indicated

Copy and cut out 2 angels for each of these shapes; 8 in all. Stick back to back ↓

Allah

← These angels have fixing holes at their bases as well as at their points because they are attached to both the Upper and Lower Struts →

↑ You could simply trace the shape outline and add your own drawing of an angel in one of the shapes

↙ Copy and cut out 2 of these shapes. Make holes at top and bottom to attach to Upper and Lower struts

Abraham

❀ Lower Strut of Seven Heavens Mobile:

Copy onto card and cut out 2 of these struts. Stick back to back for strength and to show design on both sides when Mobile is hung up. Pierce holes for hanging wire / thread as indicated

Middle Section of Seven Heavens Mobile:

Moses

Harun

Idris

Copy and cut 2 each of these roundels. Use colour & glitter to embellish them. Stick back to back

Pierce holes where shown

← Cut carefully on outer line

Mary

Joseph

John

Jesus

Pierce top and bottom ↗ for this roundel

Lower Section of Seven Heavens Mobile:

Copy and cut out 2 of these shapes. Colour and stick back to back. Pierce holes where indicated

Adam

Copy and cut 2 of these shapes. Stick back to back

With all the separate shapes cut out, coloured and stuck back to back, follow the instructions for assembling the mobile.

Muhammad

Activity 2: making a prayer rug

(This prayer rug will be a coloured design on textile cloth)

Materials:

- White or cream plain cloth (cotton or linen). (The typical size of a prayer rug is 65cm x 110cm. If you want to make a smaller one adjust the measurements maintaining the proportions.)
- Textile paints, water soluble and suitable for cottons
- Appropriate colouring brushes, water and colour-mixing containers (saucers, jar tops, etc.)
- Plastic sheeting (flattened plastic bags or similar can be used)
- Kitchen paper for cleaning brushes
- Tape measure, ruler (the longer the better), set squares
- Scissors
- Pencil and ball-point pen
- White plain paper, tracing paper, carbon paper
- Masking tape (if not available, use scotch tape)

Note:

Remember, to have a successful prayer rug, you must make sure it is complete before you remove it from the table / surface you are working on. So be sure that no one will want to use the table before you are finished!

Method:

1 Cut the cloth to the exact size you need (actual size 65cm x 110cm plus hem).
2 Hem the two long sides, fray the two short ones, and iron the edges. You may wish to do the hemming using a sewing machine, or stitch it by hand. (Good opportunities to learn these techniques).
3 Enlarge the rug design to the appropriate size on a photocopying machine, using the grid method, or make your own design.
4 Cover the work surface with plastic sheeting, securing it well to the surface with the masking tape.
5 Spread out the cloth onto the plastic sheeting and fix down, from the edges only, using the masking tape. Make sure that it is firmly spread and has no wrinkles. The best way is to secure the corners first, and then stick down the sides. The less the cloth moves the better.
6 Transfer the design onto the cloth with the aid of carbon paper, which you would place on the cloth, between it and the design. With the aid of the masking tape, fix down the carbon paper and the design. Use a ballpoint pen to trace the design, pressing firmly.
7 After tracing the pattern, remove the sheet of paper and the carbon paper. You are now ready to colour.
8 Have your textile colours, brushes, bowl of water, and the tissues nearby, but not on the cloth. Test out the colours you want to use on a scrap of the cloth. (Beware of watery colours, as they tend to spread out and spoil the work).
9 Colour in. Start either at the top of the rug and work down, or at the centre and work out (reduces risk of smudging). Place plain white paper under the wrist that holds the brush at the wrist, to avoid damaging the traced patterns on the fabric.
10 When finished colouring, leave to dry for at least 24 hours, before removing from the table.
11 Using a hot iron, iron the rug through a thick ironing cloth to fix down the paint permanently. Be careful not to let the iron directly touch the paint.
12 The rug is now complete and ready for use or hanging.

DESIGN FOR A PRAYER RUG

110 cms

65 cms

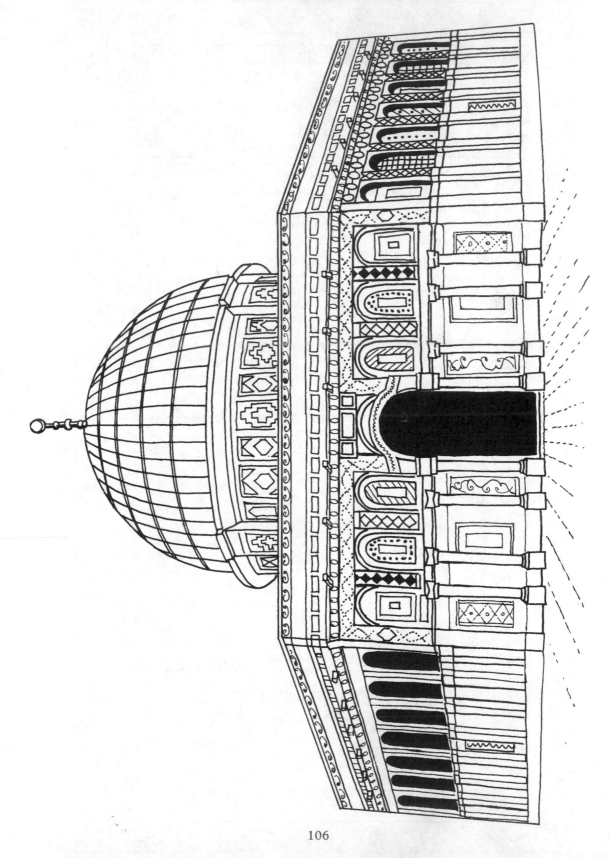

Activity 3: making a collage/mosaic of the Dome of the Rock, Jerusalem

Materials:
Mosaic set, from the 'Galt' products range.
These can be obtained from children's
educational products suppliers (see
Appendix 4)

Method:
1 Copy out the image of the Dome of the
Rock (or the simpler one overleaf).
2 Following the instructions on the pack,
make the mosaic.

Or:
Materials:
Use all the materials you can find and/or
recycle
Collect as many types of coloured paper,
card, fabrics as you can, and any other
coloured odds and ends
Gold coloured sheets or paints (for the dome)
Glue
Scotch tape
Scissors
Craft/stencil knife
Tracing paper
Thick white card for the background
Frame

Method:
1 Trace the Dome's outlines.
2 Enlarge to a suitable size worthy of the
subject, onto the sheet of card.
Enlargement can be done either using the
grid method (draw a grid over the image
and then copy by eye onto a larger grid)
or by using an enlarging photocopier.
3 Using the scraps of paper etc. decide what
you are using and where it is going.
4 Fix the coloured bits to the relevant areas
of the picture.
5 Frame the picture and hang.

Activity 4: cooking Halawat Al-Jizer (carrot halva)

Ingredients:
1 kg carrots
5 tablespoons vegetable oil
3 cups sugar
$1/2$ cup crushed walnuts
$1/2$ cup plain white flour
2 cups water, or 2 cups of carrot water
drained after boiling the carrots
$1/4 - 1/2$ cup lemon juice

Method:
1 Wash the carrots and grate or finely chop
them using a food processor, discarding
the centres if they are hard.
2 Cook the carrots in a pot of water on a
medium heat, making sure that there is
enough water to cover the carrots until
well cooked.
3 Drain the carrots thoroughly, keeping the
water for later use.
4 Heat the oil and add the carrots, mixing
them in for five minutes.
5 Add the flour to the mixture and mix in,
cooking until the flour and carrots
become golden in colour.
6 In a separate pot, on medium heat, melt
the sugar in 2 cups of the carrot water or
plain water, and stir until the syrup
thickens a little.
7 Add the lemon juice to the syrup and mix
well.
8 Pour the sugar syrup on the carrot
mixture and mix in well, keeping the
carrot pot on a low heat until the whole
mixture thickens.
9 Add the cardamom and walnuts.
10 Serve while hot. It can also be eaten cold.
You can serve it with thick cream as well.

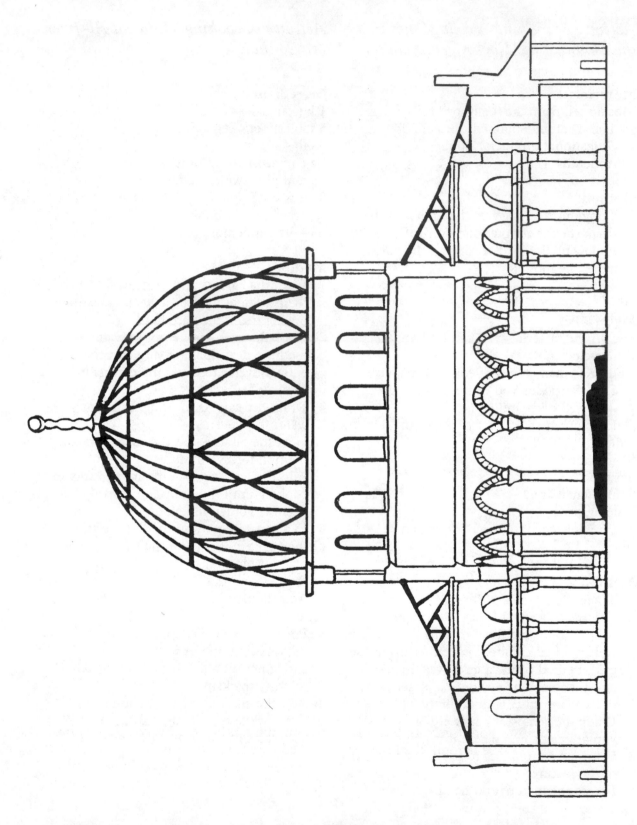

Stories about Prayer

The Night Journey of the Prophet brought the second pillar of Islam, the teaching concerning prayer. In this section several stories explore the subject of prayer.

How Did You See Me?

Muslims are instructed, in the Qur'an, to pray five times a day. While those who are able may go to a mosque to do so, others pray where they are, in their workplace or in the street. In some countries it is forbidden to walk in front of someone while they are praying.

This popular story from India illustrates the importance of the mood and spirit in which praying takes place.

Once a young woman crossed the street at a place where a Muslim was performing prayers. Without noticing, she walked in front of him, breaking the rule that forbids walking in front of a praying man. A while later the woman came back past the man, who shouted at her,

'How rude! How disrespectful! How dare you!'

'What did I do?' asked the puzzled girl.

'You walked in front of me while I was praying. That is forbidden!'

'Why is that, sir?'

'When I pray I am talking to God. It is forbidden to disturb praying by walking in front of the man who is praying.'

'Well I'm sorry, but when I walked in front of you, I didn't notice you. I was on the way to see my boyfriend and was only thinking of him, so I didn't see you. But if you were really thinking of God, then how was it that you saw me?'

Hatred and Kindness

This story about the Prophet Muhammad comes from Pakistan.

Once, when Muhammad was living in the town of Madinah, he used to pray five times a day. Often he would walk to the mosque for prayers. There was an old woman who lived near the mosque who, for some reason, did not like the Prophet. When he walked past her house on the way to prayers she would sweep dust and rubbish over him. Whenever this happened, Muhammad would turn to her, smile kindly and greet her as he would a friend. The woman never returned the greeting, and swept more dust at the Prophet.

One day, Muhammad was walking to the mosque and passed by her house. He noticed that the old woman was not there, and asked her neighbour where she had gone. They explained that she was very ill, and had to stay in bed to rest. Immediately Muhammad went to her house, cooked her a meal, swept out her house, and collected water from the well. When she saw who was helping her, the hatred for Muhammad disappeared, and in time she became a believer in Muhammad's message.

The Spout of Fortune

Before prayer at the mosque, Muslims are required to wash thoroughly so that they are fully cleansed when they pray. Many mosques have washing areas supplied with waterspouts or taps, where believers can prepare for prayer. This folktale from Iraq starts during this cleansing ritual.

Once there was a king who liked to dress up in disguise and wander the town at night. One evening he passed a weaver's hut, and heard the sound of chanting coming from inside. He peeped through the window of the hut, and saw a weaver working at his loom. As the man worked he chanted the same lines over and over again:

'I'm the one who blocked it
That's the fault I know
Once there was a tiny drip
Now even that won't flow.'

This is curious, thought the king, who knocked on the weaver's door and entered the hut.

'Excuse me,' said the king. 'I couldn't help hearing you chanting to yourself. I wonder if you could explain to me why you keep repeating those words.'

'It's just that I have no luck,' said the weaver, 'and it's all my fault!'

The weaver, whose name was Ahmed, explained that he was so poor that he could barely afford to feed his family. On good days they ate bread and salt. On bad days they ate nothing.

One day, he said, he had gone to pray at his local mosque. He went to the place where men washed before prayer, a long row of waterspouts gushing into a stone trough.

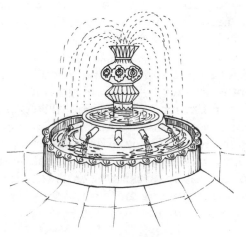

Ahmed noticed that while water was flowing strongly from most of the spouts, there was one spout where water was only coming out in slow drips.

'I wonder why that is?' Ahmed had thought to himself. At that moment God spoke in his ear, saying,

'These streams of water are like the fortunes of mankind; some have much fortune, and others little.'

'Which one is my water spout?' asked Ahmed.

God pointed to the spout where water was falling slowly, drop by drop.

Ahmed was disappointed to have such a weak spout. He took out a metal spike from his pocket and stuck it into the mouth of the spout, trying to widen it. But when Ahmed removed the spike, no water at all came out any more. The spout was completely blocked.

'So you see, all my luck has gone, and it's all my fault: I'm the one who blocked it!'

The king was surprised by Ahmed's story, and thought he'd try to prove him wrong.

The next day the king ordered that a goose be killed and plucked. Its belly was then opened, filled with gold, and sewn up again. A messenger took the goose to the weaver, telling him simply that it was a gift from a friend.

Ahmed was amazed at the gift. He had never been able to afford to buy a goose for his family. He imagined how happy they would be to taste rich goose meat. But then he thought,

'No, that would be a waste. If I sell the goose I'll be able to buy enough dry bread to last for a month. Better safe than sorry: I'll sell the goose and buy some bread.'

The weaver went to the market, sold the goose and used the money to buy a large sack of dry bread for his family.

That night the king passed by the weaver's hut and heard him singing the same sad chant.

'I'm the one who blocked it
That's the fault I know
Once there was a tiny drip
Now even that won't flow.'

The king was surprised that the weaver was not celebrating his good luck, and wondered why. The next day he sent the weaver another goose filled with gold, but again the weaver sold the goose at the market to buy some more bread. Again the king visited the weaver that night, and again heard his sad chant.

'I'm the one who blocked it
That's the fault I know
Once there was a tiny drip
Now even that won't flow.'

The next day the king sent a third goose, which again the weaver sold. When the king visited that night, and heard the same mournful chant, he lost his patience. The king summoned Ahmed to his place.

'I gave you three geese, filled with gold. Is that not enough luck to please you!' shouted the king.

'But your majesty, I sold the geese in the market and bought bread instead. My family is too poor to eat goose flesh. I didn't know there was gold inside. You see! I have no luck!

I'm the one who blocked it
That's the fault I know
Once there was a tiny drip
Now even that won't flow.'

'Stop that ridiculous chanting!' shouted the king. 'Look – I will prove you wrong. Take this bag of gold. It is for you. Let's see how your luck is now!'

The weaver took the bag of gold and

walked out of the palace in a daze, hardly able to believe his luck.

As he walked over the bridge that crossed the river in the centre of town he tripped on a rock he hadn't noticed, and dropped the gold into the river.

'Just my luck!' he thought and continued home to his loom where he continued his sad song:

'I'm the one who blocked it
That's the fault I know
Once there was a tiny drip
Now even that won't flow.'

This time, when the king heard what had happened, he gave up trying to help the weaver, and left him to his sadness and his poverty.

1   From Selected Prayers, by Jamal Badawi, Millat Book Centre, New Delhi, India

2   By the ascetic Ibrahim ibn Ad'ham, died ca. 782 AD; translated by Muhtar Holland, in: Utterances of Shaikh Abd al-Qadir al-Jilani, Al-Baz Publishing, Houston, Texas, 1992

3   From The Sublime Revelation, by Shaikh Abd al-Qadir al-Jilani, translated by Muhtar Holland, Al-Baz Publishing, Houston, Texas, 1992

4   From The Sublime Revelation, by Abd al-Qadir al-Jilani, translated by Muhtar Holland, Al-Baz Publishing, Houston, Texas, 1992

5   By Rabia Al-Adawia, 8th century Sufi saint; from Prayer & Reflection, published by An-Nisa Society, London, c.1996.)

Chapter 5

A NEW BEGINNING

Those who believed and those who suffered migration and strove for the sake of God, they have the hope of the mercy of God; and God is forgiving and merciful.

The Qur'an: *Surat Al-Baqarah*

O mankind! We have created you from male and female, and made you into nations and tribes, so that you may come to know each other. The most honoured of you in the sight of God is he who is the most righteous of you. God is All-knowing, well-versed.

The Qur'an: *Surat Al-Hujurat*

Leaving Makkah

In previous chapters we read how Muhammad was born in the holy city of Makkah into the tribe responsible for care of the holy shrine, the House of God. At the age of forty he became a prophet, teaching the words of God as spoken to him by the Angel Gabriel, later to be written as the Qur'an. He taught the worship of one God, the same God worshipped by Christians and Jews. After ten years of teaching he made a miraculous journey, flying by night to Jerusalem, meeting many of the prophets who lived before him, and ascending through seven heavenly worlds to the throne of God.

Muhammad's reputation as a wise and holy man spread, and he was often invited to help resolve conflicts in the towns and villages around Makkah. It happened that, when a dispute broke out in Madinah, a town about 300 miles from Makkah, the leaders of the two families came to Makkah asking for Muhammad's help. The Prophet explained his teachings to the leaders, and they became believers. When they returned home they passed on the message to their people. In this way the city of Madinah learned about the Prophet's teaching. Many people from Madinah visited the Prophet to learn from him, and many became teachers of Islam when they returned home. He was often invited to live in Madinah and leave Makkah.

During this period Muslims were again suffering persecution in Makkah. Muhammad instructed his followers to leave Makkah in small groups, so that the tribal chiefs would not realise that the Muslims were trying to escape. The Prophet was concerned that, if the rulers realised there was a plan for all Muslims to move to Madinah, then they would prevent it, thinking that Madinah would become a threat. By leaving gradually, however, most of his followers were able to escape before the tribal chiefs realised what was going on.

When most of Muhammad's followers had left the city, the leaders realised this and decided that the Prophet should be killed before he became too powerful. It is said that 100 young men were sent to kill the Prophet, one from each of the Makkah tribes, each with their own sword, so that no single family could be blamed for his death. They surrounded the Prophet's house and waited there, planning to kill him if he tried to leave.

Muhammad was inside his house when it was surrounded. That night God told him

that he should travel to Madinah immediately. When Muhammad left the house with a companion, the men surrounding the house did not see him. God made him invisible to his enemies, and the two walked away from the house unseen and safe, a miracle.

Muhammad asked a friend, Ali, to stay in his house and hand back the house and its contents to its owners the next day. In the morning the young men stormed the house with their swords drawn, ready to kill the Prophet, but were astonished to find only Ali in his bed.

When the Makkah leaders found out that Muhammad had escaped, they sent assassins to catch him before he reached Madinah. One night, when the assassins had nearly caught up with the Prophet, he and his companion spent the night sleeping in a cave. While they rested there a pigeon built its nest in a bush in front of the cave, and a spider spun a web across the whole of the cave entrance, so it looked as if nobody could possibly have entered the cave for weeks. When the assassins passed by the cave they saw the nest and the web and didn't bother to look inside. By this second miracle the Prophet was saved.

Muhammad and his companion, Abu Bakr, stayed in the cave for several days until the assassins had given up and gone back to Makkah. When they felt it was safe two camels were brought to them by one of Abu Bakr's servants. On these two camels the Prophet and Abu Bakr headed north towards Madinah.

Hijrah: New Year's Day

The significance of the migration to Madinah

The day when Muhammad began his journey from Makkah is called the *Hijrah*. This moment marks the beginning of the Islamic calendar, and is also New Year's Day in the Muslim year.

Muhammad's migration began a new phase of his life as a Prophet:

- The migration provided new opportunities for living a positive, productive life, away from the daily threats and hostility of a Makkah majority.

- The migrants were welcomed to Madinah and were supported by their hosts, which included teaching them a new profession, that of agriculture – an unknown skill to the people of Makkah who depended on trade and cattle.

- In Madinah Muslims were able to live by their religion in public without persecution, as they were leaders of their own community. Madinah was Islam's first independent city-state.

Where is Madinah?

Madinah lies to the north of Makkah, in the western part of the Arabian Peninsula. It is a fertile oasis rich with date palms. From early times it was one of the main agricultural settlements in the western parts of the peninsula. The name 'Madinah' means town or city.

Its proper name today is 'Al-Madinah Al-Munawara', the City of Light, lit by the presence of the Prophet in it. The Prophet chose to be buried in Madinah despite being free to go back to Makkah towards the end of his life.

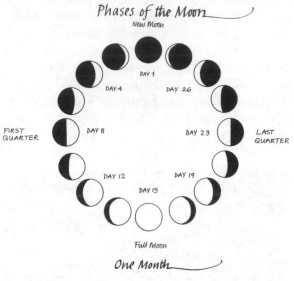

Phases of the Moon

solar calendar, each month comes earlier in the season every year. For example in 1980 the month of Ramadan started in July, in 1982 in started in June, in 1984 it started in May, in 1987 it started in April, and in 1990 it started in March.

The Muslim calendar

The Prophet's migration to Madinah marks the beginning of the spread of Arab Islamic civilization throughout the world. To mark this beginning, the Muslim 'Hijrah' calendar was adopted soon after the Prophet's death.

The Islamic Calendar is a lunar calendar, ruled by the cycle of the moon round the earth, which lasts 29 to 30 days. This calendar has 12 months, each one corresponding to one cycle of the moon. There are 354 days in every Muslim year, 11 days less than the solar calendar used by Christians, which is based on the orbit of the earth round the sun.

While summer and winter come during the same months every year in the solar calendar, this is not so for the Muslim months. Because the lunar calendar is 11 days shorter than the

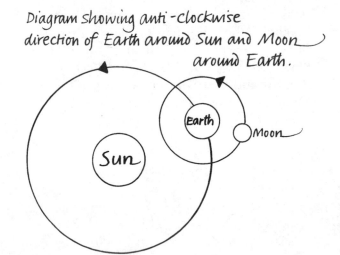

Diagram showing anti-clockwise direction of Earth around Sun and Moon around Earth.

There are various ideas about why the lunar calendar was used:

- The desert Arabs made their living from trade, travel and cattle, rather than permanent agriculture, for which the solar calendar might be more useful.

- For desert travellers, the phases of the moon offer a clear and practical way of measuring time.

- Most of the time it is summer in the Arabian Desert – the other seasons are very short and not particularly important to the inhabitants.

The Islamic Months are:
  Muharram
  Safar
  Rabi' al-Awal
  Rabi' ath-Thani
  Jamada' al-Awal
  Jamada' ath-Thani
  Rajab
  Sha'ban
  Ramadan *(the fasting month)*
  Shawwal
  Dhul Qa'dah
  Dhul Hijjah *(the pilgrimage month)*

There are seven days in the Islamic week, which correspond directly to the Western weekdays, except that for Muslims the week begins on a Saturday and ends on a Friday, the holy day in the week.

The Arabic names of the days of the week are:
  al-Sabt (Saturday)
  al-Ahad (Sunday)
  al-Ithnain (Monday)
  ath-Thalatha' (Tuesday)
  al-Arba' (Wednesday)
  al-Khamis (Thursday)
  al-Jumuah (the congregational day, Friday)

(Note: the Arabic names for Sunday, Monday, Tuesday, Wednesday and Thursday correspond to the numbers 1, 2, 3, 4 and 5 respectively. This is because Sunday is the first day after the Sabbath (Saturday), Monday is the second day after the Sabbath, and so on.)

A day in the Muslim calendar:
Each day is divided into five periods that mark the 5 times when Muslims pray:
  Fajr (Dawn)
  Zuhur (Midday)
  'Asr (Afternoon)
  Maghreb (Sunset)
  'Isha (Night)

Unlike the solar calendar day, which lasts an exact 24 hour period, starting and ending at midnight, the Islamic lunar day starts and ends with the Fajr (dawn).

Below, a Palestinian Muslim describes the way that the Muslim Calendar provides regular opportunities for pause and prayer, a break from the hustle and bustle of daily life:

- Every day there are five times when a Muslim may pray and experience a few minutes of peace.

- Once a week, on Fridays, a Muslim may go to the mosque for prayer and a chance to listen to holy teachings.

- Once a year, the month of Ramadan provides an opportunity for a fasting, purification and prayer.

- Once in a lifetime (or a few times) a Muslim may make a pilgrimage to Makkah, an opportunity to reflect on his/her life as a whole and experience community with Muslims from all over the world.

In most of the Muslim World the Islamic New Year is celebrated on the first day of Muharram. On that day men and boys go to the mosque in the evening to pray and attend the religious celebrations. These usually consist of the recitations of the Qur'an, religious chanting, and prayers. At home, family gatherings take place in celebration of this event.

Activity Ideas

✦ Making a calendar with lunar and solar months

✦ Making greeting cards for the New Year

✦ Making ceramic wall plaques depicting the desert journey

✦ Cooking Aish Al-Saria (Palace Sweet Bread)

Activity 1: making a calendar with lunar and solar months

This is a flexible activity. The calendar sheets can be simply coloured in with pens, or more creatively coloured by using a combination of coloured paper, textiles and pens.

As each sheet of the calendar covers three months, this activity can be spread out over the year: more advanced craft techniques used as the child's skills progress.

The calendar's four sheets (see following pages) cover the four quarters of the year, and explore the phases of the moon, musical instruments, flowers, and maps of the world.

Materials:
White card or thick sheets of paper (A3 size), you will need 6 sheets
Colouring pens
Coloured paper (scraps from coloured magazines, wrapping paper etc. are useful for this activity)
Scraps of textiles, felt, woollen thread, cotton etc.
Scissors
Glue
Pencil
Ruler

Method:
1 Cut the card/paper to the appropriate size.
2 Enlarge and copy the design for each of the calendar pages on to the card/paper. Enlargement can be by eye using a grid, or using an enlargement photocopier.
3 Fill in the blanks and the calendar dates as you see appropriate.
4 Using the colouring pens, textile scraps and coloured paper, fill in the calendar designs.
5 When complete, hang on the wall. You might like to frame the calendar in a simple clip-frame, which consists of a sheet of glass, backing, and metal clips, without a wooden frame.

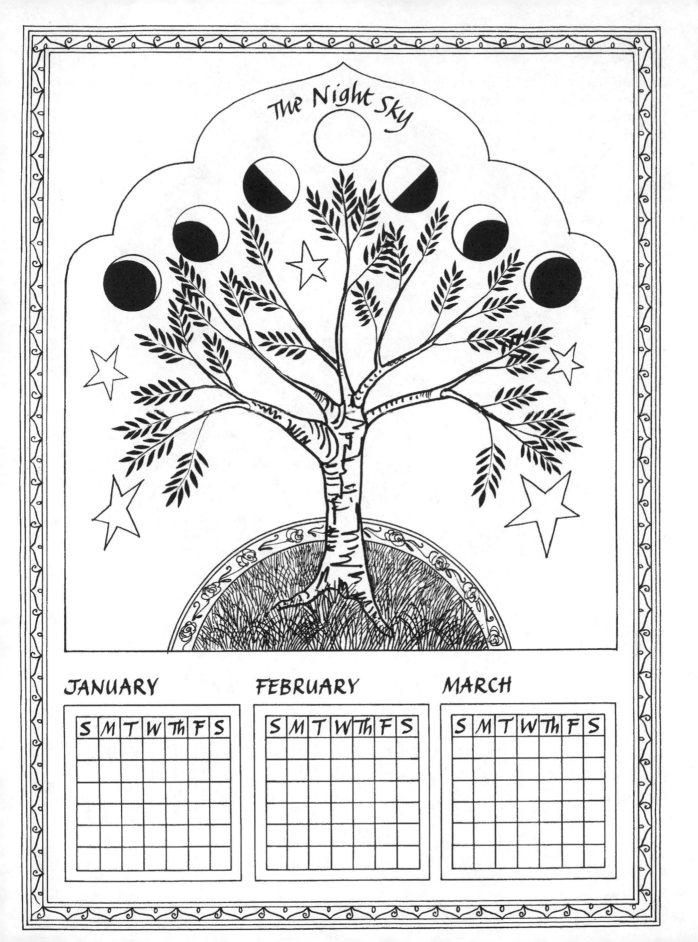

The Night Sky

JANUARY

S	M	T	W	Th	F	S

FEBRUARY

S	M	T	W	Th	F	S

MARCH

S	M	T	W	Th	F	S

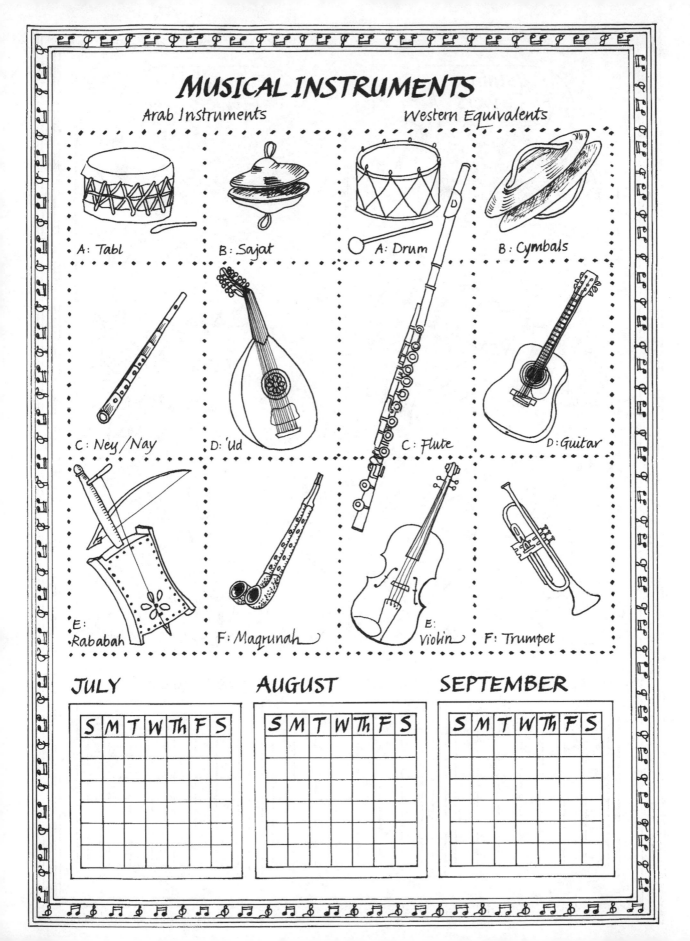

Islamic Flowers

European Flowers

Carnation

Rose

Tulip

OCTOBER

S	M	T	W	Th	F	S

NOVEMBER

S	M	T	W	Th	F	S

DECEMBER

S	M	T	W	Th	F	S

Activity 2: making greeting cards for the New Year

This activity can be simplified for small children by applying the designs straight onto the card and colouring them in.

Choose one of these designs for transferring to the soft metal sheet

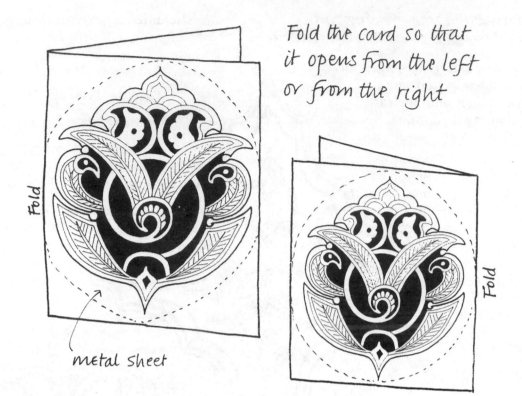

Fold the card so that it opens from the left or from the right

Fold

metal sheet

Fold

Write a New Year Greeting inside the card, using Arabic or English script as shown below :

Happy New Year

عام سعيد

كل عام وانتم بخير

Congratulations for the New Year

Materials:

Sheets of card, any colour that complements the colour of the metal sheets

Soft metal sheets. These can be obtained from art and crafts equipment suppliers. They come in several colours and sizes. You can also recycle the aluminium seals of large tins of coffee, coffee whitener, etc.

Embossing tools. You can get these from the same suppliers, or you can make your own by using things about the house, which may provide the same effects. Such items as pencils with rubber ends, inkless ballpoint pens, blunt fruit knives, thick plastic or metal knitting needles, the handles of wooden spoons, etc.

Pencil and ballpoint pen

Scissors

Ruler

Tracing paper

Glue or scotch tape

A soft plastic pad for pressing/embossing the metal sheet on (a computer mouse-pad, or a chopping board covered with a thin towel and paper sheets)

Method:

1 Trace one of the designs onto tracing paper.
2 Cut out the size of metal sheet you need (leave a little extra space on all sides which you can trim with scissors at the end).
3 Place the metal sheet on the mat, and place the pattern you have traced on the metal sheet.
4 Using the embossing tools, or other pointed tool, transfer the pattern onto the metal sheet by pressing over the lines.
5 To raise (puff up) parts of the design, turn the metal sheet over onto the reverse side and press the areas to be raised using a rounded edge, like the rubber edge of the pencil, or the rounded edge of the wooden spoon handle.
6 You can etch or scratch parts of the pattern

to create different textures by using the blunt edge of the fruit knife.
7 Trim the edges of the metal.
8 Fold the card you want to use to the right size.
9 Stick the metal pattern onto the card by using glue or scotch tape.

Activity 3: making ceramic wall plaques depicting the desert journey

The figures you can make include: camels, saddle bags full of goods, travellers, date palm trees, sandy hills of the desert, and anything else associated with travelling through the desert.

Materials:

A pack of modelling clay. This comes in several colours. If you chose white or brown, you would be able to colour the clay appropriately. 'DAS Pronto' is a white, air-hardening modelling material which can be purchased from art materials and equipment shops.

Suitable colours for painting on modelling clay. Ceramic gloss colours (the type that dry at room temperature) can be purchased from art materials and equipment shops. 'Pebeo' make a range of cold ceramic colours, and 'Humbrol' make a range of cold enamel paints, all of which dry without the need for firing.

Varnish suitable for modelling clay

Brushes and thinners for the paints

Modelling tools suitable for the clay. These are made of plastic or wood. Three different shapes are adequate.

Rolling pin, knife, and other simple tools to help in shaping the modelling clay (thick knitting needle, pencil with a rubber end, etc.)

Sheets of white card to copy the patterns

Pencil

Scissors

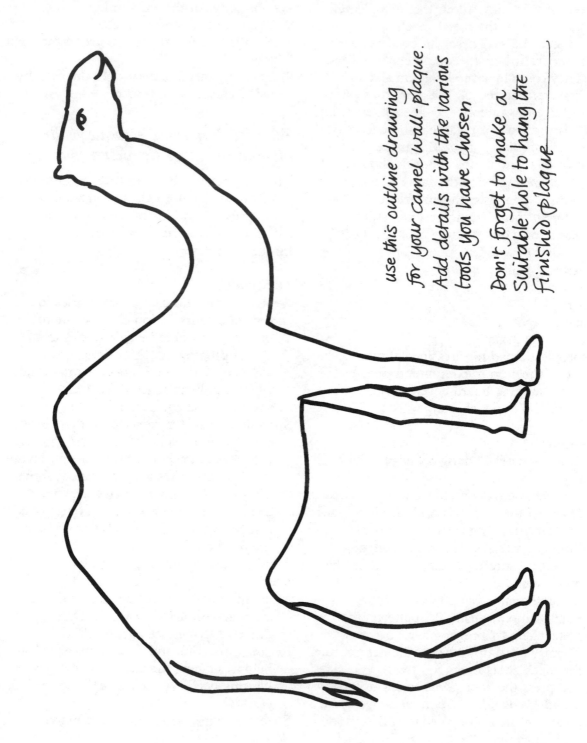

use this outline drawing
for your camel wall-plaque.
Add details with the various
tools you have chosen

Don't forget to make a
suitable hole to hang the
finished plaque

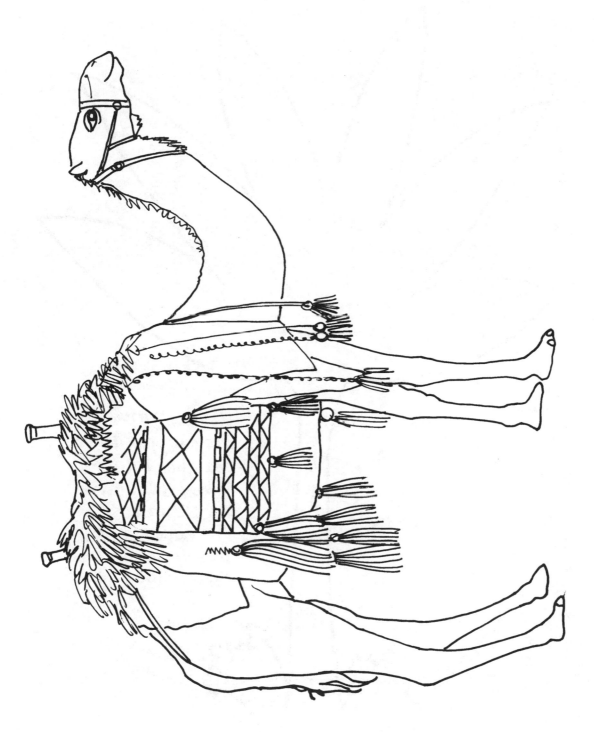

Use this outline to cut out your palm tree, then fill in some details from the picture.
The hanging hole for this design could be somewhere central

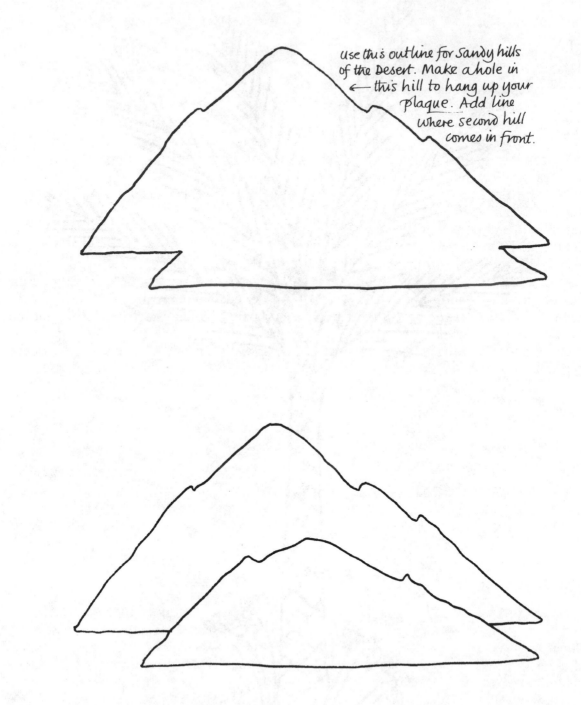

Use this outline for sandy hills of the Desert. Make a hole in ← this hill to hang up your plaque. Add line where second hill comes in front.

Method:

1 Copy the shapes onto the white card and cut out. These are your patterns.
2 Role out the modelling clay, at a thickness of 0.7cm – 1cm maximum.
3 Placing the card pattern on the rolled out modelling clay and using the knife, cut out the shapes of the caravan figures.
4 Using the other tools, mark and shape each of the figures.
5 Make a hole at the top of each figure, big enough to insert a nail for hanging on the wall (0.5cm diameter is an appropriate size for the hole).
6 Leave to dry, as specified on the modelling clay pack instructions.
7 Colour the figures. Leave to dry. You may wish to varnish the figures without colouring them.
8 Varnish the figures and leave to dry.
9 Hang on the wall. (If you have forgotten to make holes for hanging before the clay shapes have dried, you can still hang them by positioning two or three nails in the lower corners of each of the plaques to secure them on the wall).

Activity 4. cooking Aish Al-Saria (Palace Sweet Bread)

This is a popular Egyptian sweet dish.

Ingredients:

For the sugar syrup:
3 cups sugar
3 cups water
1 tablespoon rosewater

For the sweet bread:
1 loaf of bread, medium sliced, white or brown
3 cups full-fat dried milk powder
$4^1/2$ cups water
4 tablespoons corn flour
1 cup sugar

200g double cream
1 cup crushed mixed nuts, preferably: walnuts, almonds, pistachios, pine nuts
1 tablespoon rosewater

Method:

The sugar syrup:

1 Add the sugar to a pot on the stove, stirring it until it browns.
2 Add the water gradually while continuing to stir the mixture. Continue until all the sugar has dissolved.
3 Remove from the heat and add the rosewater.
4 Leave to cool.

The sweet bread:

1 If not sliced, slice the loaf, and remove the outer edges and crust.
2 Prepare a baking-tray type of dish, not too shallow.
3 Dip the slices of loaf, one at a time, in the sugar syrup, and set the slices of loaf evenly along the bottom of the dish, packing them in firmly.

The nut mixture:

1 In a separate pot, add the $4^1/2$ cups of water, and gradually mix in the powdered milk, corn flour and sugar.
2 Turn on the heat and stir the mixture until all the ingredients blend and become thickened like custard.
3 While still on the heat, add the rosewater and mix in.
4 Add the cream and mix in.
5 Add three quarters of the crushed nuts, mixing in and stirring for a few minutes.
6 Remove the pot from the stove and pour its contents all over the dish of loaf slices, making sure that all get covered evenly.
7 Use the remaining quarter of crushed nuts to decorate the dish.
8 Serve hot, or chilled.

Stories about Travel and Danger

Muhammad's journey from Makkah to Madinah was dangerous and difficult. In this section we offer three stories from West Africa and one from Malaysia, on the theme of danger and journeys.

Why Men have no Tails

Long ago, when the world had just begun, all people had tails hanging down behind them. Tails were considered very important. People took great pride in their long, shiny tails and would show them off at every opportunity.

In those days there was a great and famous hunter. He had killed so many wild and dangerous animals he was given the name King-of-all-Hunters.

King-of-all-Hunters had a son whose name was Amir, the Prince-of-Hunters. When Amir was old enough to be married, he went to his father and said:

'Father, there is a girl in this village whom I wish to marry. Will you give your permission?'

His father decided to give his son a test, to see if he was ready for marriage:

'Amir, if you are to marry then you must prove you are ready. I will set you a test – pass it and I will give my permission. When I was young I killed all the savage and wild creatures in the forest – all, that is, except one. There is a monster with seven heads, nine mouths, thirteen arms and seventeen legs. It has the strength of an elephant and the speed of a leopard. Go out into the forest and kill this creature, then you may marry. Will you do it?'

The son smiled and said he would.

The next day Amir waved goodbye to his family and set off into the forest. He walked for three days and three nights, eating only nuts and berries. On the third evening he came to an old hut. Outside was an old woman washing her cooking pots in the stream.

'Where are you going in such a hurry?' asked the old woman.

'I seek the monster with seven heads, nine mouths, thirteen arms and seventeen legs. It has the strength of an elephant and the speed of a leopard, and I will hunt it!' he called out bravely.

'Well you'd better eat something first,' she replied, 'or you'll be too weak to fight. Here, have some food.'

Amir ate well. When he had finished the old woman gave him a clay pot with a narrow neck, and told him to wash it. He took it down to the stream. As he was washing it, the pot broke into two halves and out fell an egg, a stone and some dry grass.

The old woman grinned when she saw what had happened:

'I am glad you broke the pot!' she said. 'The things inside are for you. If you are in danger, drop the egg, then the grass, and last the stone. Do that and you will be helped!'

Amir thanked the old woman and continued on his journey.

The next day he came to a very dark, thick part of the forest. When he felt his spine tingling and his hands shaking, he knew there was danger close by. Suddenly, there in front of him, appearing as if from nowhere, was the terrible creature with seven heads, nine mouths, thirteen arms and seventeen legs. Amir took his knife and rushed at the monster, cutting and slashing at its huge body. They fought without rest for a day and a night and another day, but in the end Amir was victorious. He turned around and started walking home, thinking of the girl he planned to marry.

The next day he was walking the road towards home when a great beast came up behind him, more terrible than the one he had killed. The creature was furious, with steam hissing from its mouths and fire blazing from its eyes. It was the mother of the creature that Amir had killed.

Amir began to run, but the monster was faster. Soon it was right behind him, and stretched out its arms to grab him. Just then he took the egg from his pocket and dropped it on the ground. Immediately a vast lake formed between Amir and the monster. When Amir looked behind, the monster was just a tiny speck in the distance on the other side of the lake.

As Amir ran home, the monster ran around the lake and was soon close behind him again, reaching out to grab him. This time the hunter dropped the dry grass behind him, and a thick dark forest sprung up between him and the monster. It was too thick to walk through, so the monster had to go round the side of the forest. Soon the monster caught up again, but this time Amir dropped the stone, creating a high mountain range too high for the monster to climb.

Finally, Amir reached the door of his father's house, with the monster right behind

him. As he opened the door and was about to step inside, the creature reached out and grabbed hold of his tail. Terrified, Amir jumped into the house, leaving his tail in the monster's hand.

Back in his father's house, the house of the King-of-the-Hunters, the young man was safe, and he told his father what had happened.

'Look father,' he said, 'the creature has taken my tail!'

The King-of-All-Hunters looked, and sure enough, the tail was gone. He gave his son permission to marry.

'One day,' said his father,' you will be a great hunter, because you know when to fight, and when to run.'

Since then, Amir's children and grandchildren were born without tails. Nobody mocked them, however, because they respected the courage and wisdom of Amir. Gradually, fewer and fewer men had tails, until today they are very rare indeed!

But if it hadn't been for Amir, we would all still have tails to this day!

Mullum the Warrior

Once there was a soldier called Mullum. He was the greatest and bravest warrior in the land, respected by his friends and feared by his enemies. Mullum's country was at war with the neighbouring king, but thanks to Mullum's bravery their country was never invaded.

One day Mullum went out hunting on his great black warhorse, but that day there were no animals to be seen, and Mullum travelled further and further away from home into a forest. After a while he grew tired, and, dismounting from his horse, he fell asleep under a tree, leaving the horse tethered on the path.

While Mullum was sleeping some wood-cutters came along the path and, seeing the fine black horse, decided to take it to the king as a gift. They untied it and led it to the king's palace, not noticing Mullum still asleep under the tree.

When the king saw the horse, he recognised it from previous battles.

'This is the horse of Mullum, our enemy!' he declared. 'Without it he will not be able to fight so well. It is good that we keep it here!'

The king ordered that the horse be locked up inside the royal stables and treated well.

A while later Mullum woke up and found that his horse had gone. He followed the tracks of the horse through the forest, out into a valley, and all the way to the king's palace. When he saw the palace Mullum realised he was in the country of his enemies. Nevertheless, he sent a boy to the king with a message stating that he, Mullum, was searching for his horse.

When the king got the message he came out to speak with Mullum, inviting him into the palace to eat and rest. The king did not offer to give up the horse, but neither did he refuse, and so Mullum agreed and entered the palace, eating, washing and sleeping in fine rooms as the most honoured guest.

In the night Mullum dreamed of a beautiful young girl. In the morning he woke up and she was standing at the foot of his bed.

'Who are you?' he asked, hardly believing his eyes.

'I am the daughter of the king,' she said.

Mullum and the princess talked for a while and, delighted by her beauty, Mullum asked her to marry him.

'Only with my father's permission,' she replied, and skipped away back to her own rooms.

When Mullum asked for permission the king agreed, saying:

'You may marry her, but only if you agree never to fight against me. If a war ever starts between our countries then my daughter must return to me. In this way let it be a marriage for peace.'

Mullum agreed to the condition, and they were married. When the wedding was over he rode back home with the princess and they lived happily for a while in Mullum's country.

Six months later war broke out between Mullum's country and that of the princess' father. Because of the agreement, the princess had to go home and leave her husband, even though she was going to have a baby. Before she left, Mullum gave her a tiny red leather envelope on a piece of string.

'Hang this around our child's neck,' he said, 'and he will be protected from danger.'

Soon after the princess returned home she gave birth to a baby boy, calling him Sahbi (meaning friend). He always wore that red leather envelope around his neck. As Sahbi grew older he became a strong and brave fighter and was soon famous in his own land for his courage and skill.

One day he asked his mother who his father was, and she told him the story, saying that Mullum was now fighting with their enemies, against their country. When Sahbi heard this he vowed to conquer that country, so that his own father the soldier might be made king there.

Sahbi gathered together a great army and invaded Mullum's country. This time Mullum and his soldiers were no match for the invaders and in every battle more and more of Mullum's men were killed. Sahbi fought with great passion, driven on by the idea that he would win a country for his own father. He did not realise that Mullum himself was fighting, leading the opposing army.

Finally Mullum and Sahbi met on the battlefield, as leaders of the two armies, and fought each other in hand-to-hand combat. Sahbi asked Mullum his name, but Mullum said nothing, fighting in silence. The battle lasted for hours, but finally Mullum pushed his son to the ground and slashed him across the chest. At that moment he noticed the red leather pouch and realised what he had done.

As Sahbi died he called out:

'Now all my plans are ruined. I came here to bring glory to my father Mullum, but now I am dead I can do nothing more. I will never even meet him!'

'That is not so, my son!' cried Mullum, 'you have met him and made him proud!'

Sahbi died in his father's arms, and Mullam vowed – there and then – never to fight in battle again. For the rest of his life he did everything he could to bring peace between his country and his neighbours. When peace was achieved he was reunited with his wife. Together they raised a family, and were never separated by war again.

The Boy in the Drum

Once there was a boy, Hanifi, who wanted to be a man.

'I will go hunting!' he said to his parents.

'No, you are too young!' said his mother.

'No, you are too young!' said his father.

But Hanifi went hunting anyway. He travelled deep into the forest looking for animals to hunt.

Soon he was lost, hungry and frightened. He saw a hut, with an old man sitting by a fire outside the hut.

'Hello old man, may I join you?' he called out.

'Yes, yes, come here my boy, come here. Come and sit inside this pot, where it is nice and cool.'

The boy climbed into a big clay pot, but as soon as he was in there the old man stuck an animal skin over the top of the pot, trapping the boy inside.

'Now you must sing for your supper!' he called, beating a loud rhythm on top of the skin, 'sing, boy, sing!'

Inside the drum the little boy began to sing:

'Stuck in a pot
Happy I am not
Help me, help me
I'm just a little tot.'

The old man started visiting the villages and playing his drum. When the people heard the drum singing like a child they thought it was marvellous that the drum could sing, and gave the old man food and money so that he became rich.

In the evenings he would slip small amounts of food and water into the drum for Hanifi to eat, but he never let him out. Day after day, again and again, Hanifi would sing the same song

'Stuck in a pot
Happy I am not

Help me, help me
I'm just a little tot.'

A long while later the old man visited the
village of Hanifi's parents. When his parents
heard the sound of the singing drum they
knew it was their son inside. The boy's father
pushed the old man aside and cut open the
drum skin. The boy jumped out and hugged
both his parents.

After that Hanifi never went out alone
into the forest until his parents said he was
ready …or did he?

How Mouse Deer Saved Buffalo from the Crocodile

Salaam means peace in Arabic, and is a
common greeting when Muslims meet. In
Malaysia Salaam the Mouse Deer is a
popular folktale character. Mouse Deer uses
his wit and wisdom to avoid the many perils
of the jungle. Here he saves one animal but
makes an enemy of another. A mouse deer is
an animal rather like a deer, but much
smaller, about the size of a large mouse.

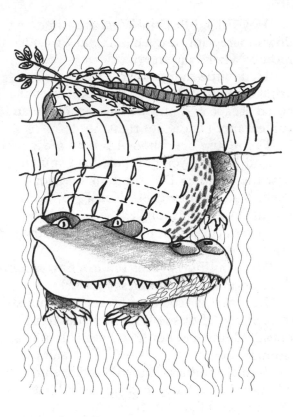

Once, Salaam the mouse deer was
travelling through the forest searching
for fresh fruit to eat, when he came to a
river. Now it happened that a few moments
before a great tree had fallen down into the
river, pinning the tail of a huge and ancient
crocodile to the riverbed. Salaam watched
the huge, wrinkled beast writhing in pain
under the weight of the tree. A little while
later Buffalo came walking along the path
right past the fallen tree.

Crocodile opened his strong deadly jaws,
and called out in the sweetest voice he could
manage:

'Hey! Friend Buffalo! Good strong and
mighty friend! Would you be so kind as to

use your great strength and lift this tree, just
a little, from my tail?'

Buffalo looked carefully, and slowly at
Crocodile, and in particular at his sharp teeth.

'H'mmm, friend Crocodile, how can I lift
that log, I have no arms!'

'No, friend Buffalo, but you have horns. A
little log should be no problem to a mighty
beast like you.'

Buffalo liked being called a mighty beast.
He knelt down under the tree, dug his horns
into the trunk and, heaving with all his
strength, lifted the tree up just enough so that
Crocodile could slip out. The first thing that
Crocodile did was close his jaws with a great
snap around the leg of Buffalo.

'No!' bellowed Buffalo. 'No friend
Crocodile, this will not do! I help you with
kindness and you repay me like this. This is
not right!'

Just then little mouse deer Salaam jumped
up and shouted out:

137

'Hey Friend Buffalo! What are you doing down there with your leg in friend Crocodile's mouth! What's the story?'

'Hello little mouse deer. I am here unjustly. I lifted the tree so friend Crocodile could escape and now he has caught me and will eat me. That is not right!'

The mouse deer shook his head sadly. 'Friend Buffalo, you old fool, don't you know how the world is? Do you think that good deeds lead to more good deeds? No, that is not the way in this jungle!'

Salaam called out to an old dog on the other side of the river:

'Hey you! Furry face! Tell me, how is it in the world? How is kindness repaid?'

'Kindness is repaid with cruelty,' whined the old dog. 'I was faithful and kind to my master all my life, but now I am old and tired, he has thrown me out to die alone in the forest. Kindness is repaid by cruelty!'

'You see, Buffalo,' said Salaam, 'That's how the world is. You should know that!'

An old basket was floating down the river and Salaam called out to it: 'Hey there old basket. How is it in the world? Is kindness repaid by kindness?'

'Oh no,' replied the basket. 'In the world kindness is repaid with unkindness. I was my master's basket. I served him for years, carrying everything that needed carrying, but now that I'm worn out, he threw me away in the river, just like that!'

Salaam turned back to the crocodile:

'Friend Crocodile, I still find your story hard to believe. That tree trunk is very big and heavy. I can't believe Buffalo really lifted the trunk. Show me again! Friend Crocodile, be so kind as to let go of Buffalo's leg for a minute so we can see if he can repeat this great deed!'

Crocodile opened his jaws, and Buffalo, sensing that Salaam was up to something, dug his horns back into the tree trunk and lifted it up.

'Friend Crocodile!' continued Salaam. 'Just let me see how things were when this story began. Be so kind as to put your tail back underneath the tree, the way it was. Let me see how it was!'

As soon as the foolish old crocodile had put his tail under the tree, Buffalo let go of the tree, and it fell back onto Crocodile's tail.

'AAWW!' He cried, 'AAWW, lift it again, friend Buffalo, lift it again!'

Crocodile twisted and struggled but could not get out from under the tree.

'Let that be a lesson for you, friend Crocodile' scolded Salaam, who scampered off across the tree truck to the other side of the river in search of fresh fruit.'

'A curse on you and your tribe!' shouted Crocodile. 'Whenever a mouse deer comes down to the river to drink, my people will be waiting for you and will gobble you up!'

And from that day to this, whenever a crocodile sees a mouse deer, he tries to kill it. But usually the mouse deer are too quick and smart to be caught!

Chapter 6

ESTABLISHING COMMUNITY

Ramadan is the month in which the Qur'an was revealed as a guide to mankind, and as evidence for the true religion. So whoever of you witnesses the beginning of this month, should fast it. He who is ill or on a journey, can fast a similar number of days later on. God intends easiness for you and does not want you to suffer difficulty to complete the prescribed period; and to magnify Him for His guidance, and be thankful to Him.

The Qur'an: *Surat Al-Baqarah*

Life in Madinah

In previous chapters we read how Muhammad was born in the holy city of Makkah, and began to receive God's revelations at the age of forty. He preached a message calling for the worship of one God, and was opposed by the pagan tribes of Makkah. Muhammad and his followers suffered persecution in Makkah. Eventually the Prophet left there and moved to the town of Madinah.

The prophet arrived in Madinah on a Friday and, amid great celebrations, offered prayers and delivered his first sermon at the Madinah mosque. A popular Islamic song celebrates this journey to Madinah Al-Nabi, the city of the Prophet. Its translation is given below.

> O the full moon rose over us
> From the valley of Wada
> And we owe it to show gratitude
> Where the call is to Allah
>
> O you who were raised amongst us
> Coming with a word to be obeyed
> You have brought our city nobility
> Welcome best caller to God's way

All of the clans welcomed him and invited him to be their guest and live in their part of the town. Muhammad wanted to be fair to everyone, and not be seen to favour one family. He announced that he would live wherever his camel chose to stop, believing that God's will would guide his camel. He let his camel walk freely around the town, until finally it knelt down on land belonging to his mother's clan. There he ordered that a mosque be built there, and other rooms where he lived.

In Madinah Muhammad was the leader of the Muslim community. His immediate problem was to deal with the many Muslims who had recently arrived from other towns and had no property or way to make a living. Muhammad asked local Muslims to show generosity to the refugees, and treat them as if they were their own brothers. In this way the newcomers were welcomed and cared for until they could make their own living.

In Madinah there were both Muslims and Jews, and the Prophet decreed that all should be free to practise their own religion without interference. This was respected by both Jews and Muslims.

During his life in Madinah, the prophet established two more of the pillars of Islam: a charitable tax for the poor (Zakah), and the practice of fasting in the month of Ramadan (Sawm). Zakah means it is the duty of all Muslims who are able to do so, to give a proportion of their wealth to the poor and needy. This is based on the principle of helping the needy, which runs throughout Islam.

The practice of fasting was introduced during the month of Ramadan: no food, drink or sexual contact was permitted between sunrise and sunset during the month, in order to achieve control of the senses and purification of the body. This teaching built on an existing tradition of fasting and prayer during the month of Ramadan.

Another new practice was a change to the direction of prayer. In common with Jews, Muslims had until then prayed facing towards Jerusalem, the place of the prophet's ascension during the Night Journey. Now Muslims were instructed to face Makkah when praying, the site of the holiest shrine, the House of God.

While the first Islamic state was being established in Madinah, armies were sent from Makkah to try to defeat Muhammad. There were several battles in which Muslims were hugely outnumbered but nevertheless were victorious. Muhammad ordered that all prisoners of war should be treated humanely, which was not the usual practice at that time.

In one of the battles, when a force of ten thousand soldiers marched to Madinah, the Muslims dug a deep ditch around the whole city so that it could be defended. The result was a one-month siege, after which the army retreated and the Muslims were finally able to make peace with the Makkah tribes. In this way a period of peace and prosperity began for the people of Madinah.

Ramadan and the Id Feast at the End of Ramadan

Fasting during the month of Ramadan

The month of Ramadan is the ninth month of the Islamic calendar. It starts the morning after the new moon, and ends with the next new moon. The fast, lasting for the whole month, is a daily fast, starting at daybreak and ending at sunset. During that period Muslims refrain from eating, drinking, smoking and sexual intercourse. The evening time is spent eating, resting, and in meditation. Throughout the month, extra prayers and meditation are conducted in all the mosques.

Ramadan had been a special month well before the birth of Islam. The Arabs in the Arabian Peninsula went to spiritual retreats and fasted during that month, as did Muhammad himself. He was on such a retreat when the Angel Gabriel first appeared to him to deliver the first verses of the Qur'an, on the 27th of Ramadan 610 AD (see Chapter 3).

Why fast?

Fasting is a real test of a person's self control and discipline. For Muslims the practice of fasting helps increase awareness of God. Muslim children are introduced to fasting in a gradual manner. Children from the age of seven are encouraged to have a go at fasting. Some children will drink liquids throughout the day but will not eat. Some fast for half a day and end their fast at lunchtime.

The Girls' Fast

In Iraq there is a special day for teaching children to fast. This day is called the Girls' Fast, held on the last Wednesday in the month of Rajab. This is a half-day fast for children, to teach them perseverance and as practice for fasting in the month of Ramadan.

The fast starts in the morning and ends at noon. A food tray is prepared for this occasion, and served at lunchtime.

During the morning the children refrain from any food and drink, and will be quite excited and looking forward to noon, when they will have a meal. On this occasion an adult in the family usually entertains the children with a specific story:

The Woodcutter's Daughter

Once upon a time there was a poor woodcutter who had a lovely young daughter. As they were very poor, the girl, although still a child, was sent to work in a wealthy man's house as a servant. Her mistress treated the girl harshly, giving her hard work and little food.

One day, the mistress of the house woke up to find that she was missing a valuable necklace. The mistress, unable to find her piece of jewellery, and not knowing how she could have lost this necklace, accused the woodcutter's daughter of stealing it. The poor girl was innocent, but her mistress did not believe her.

The girl was sad and lonely and prayed to God for help. She vowed to fast until her innocence was proven.

Later that day, at noon-time, a crow flew in through one of the windows of the house, returning the necklace into her mistress' hand. There was great surprise and excitement in the house, and the woodcutter's daughter's innocence was proven. The girl was most grateful for God's help.

Since this time, the 'Girls' Fast' has become a tradition for Muslim children in Iraq. While the story is being told, the storyteller stops after each section and the children repeat this chant:

> God gives his mercy,
> To us and to you
> Just as he gave it
> To the young girl too!

The dawn crier

In many Muslim communities, a dawn crier (musaharati) works throughout the month of Ramadan. His main duty is to walk round the neighbourhood just before dawn, drumming, singing and calling out for people to rise and get prepared for the next day's fast.

A typical chant might be:

> Wake up you sleepers
> And give praise to God
> Ramadan is a time for giving
> Wake and give praises to God

Id-ul-Fitr

On the first day of Shawal, the month following Ramadan, the Muslim community celebrates the Id, the festival for ending the fast. This is one of the two main Muslim feasts which are prescribed in the Qur'an. In most countries celebration includes: going to the mosque for the Id prayers, dressing up in new clothes, visiting family and relatives, gifts to children, and rich food. Often the celebrations go on for two or three days.

The following are based on accounts of Ramadan and Id by Muslims from several parts of the world:

Iraq

Throughout Ramadan, at sunset every afternoon, as the mosque caller calls people to prayers, people break their fast with a glass of yoghurt and several dates (this follows the Prophet's custom when breaking his fast). Supper is usually lentil soup and other savoury dishes.

The rest of the evening is spent with members of the family and friends. Prayers and recitations of the Qur'an are carried out, and the men go out to the local coffee shops to meet up with friends and neighbours. Games like dominoes, chess, and backgammon are often played. In Baghdad there is a team game called Al-Mehabis which is specifically only played during Ramadan.

At some of the coffee houses there will be a storyteller, telling tales from local folklore, Islamic history, and the Thousand and One Nights stories.

From midnight, every night during Ramadan, the dawn crier (musaharati) goes round the neighbourhood's streets, drumming on his drum and calling out for people to wake up and prepare for the last meal before daybreak. The musaharati is rewarded for his work at the end of Ramadan with gifts from the neighbourhood.

People wake up and prepare a meal that will help them cope through the next day's

fasting. Typical foods include boiled rice, bread, cheese, eggs, and juices made of dried fruits.

Id-ul-Fitr is also known as the small Id, as it only last for three days. During the Id new clothes are bought for all the members of the family, money is given to children, people visit relatives and neighbours, and all sorts of sweet and savoury foods are cooked.

Bangladesh

During the first day of the Id-ul-Fitr, Muslims are expected to wash and wear new or good clean clothes. Men wear perfume and everyone eats a little something sweet. Everyone goes to a large open space for prayer called the 'Idga'. It is a time to visit friends and neighbours, as well as the needy in the community, and make peace with enemies. At the mosques, Islamic stories are told to the community.

Before the feast new clothes are distributed by the wealthy to the poor, so that they can wear them on the first day of the Id. People are encouraged to remember the poor in their communities and give them from what they can afford. It is the duty of every Muslim to help all the poor. During the holiday period, particular attention is given to helping the poor within the Muslim community, so that they can share in the celebrations.

Palestine

A Palestinian woman describes her childhood memories of Ramadan in northern Palestine:

'In Ramadan the meals were special, because we would sit in front of the food and wait and wait and wait, and then it was wonderful to eat after that. As a child it was wonderful to fast because we got respect from teachers and adults; and people would not make you work too hard at school or home. It made us feel special. I used to fast most years.

The Id festival was a time to get in touch with family and relatives' news. We spent a lot of time talking about that; and then when people from refugee camps in Jordan came, we would take special care of them and sit and hear their stories of their troubles, and we would give them financial help.

In those days there was no habit of travelling outside the village. Everything happened there, inside the village. I had five sisters living in other houses, and it was hard to know which one to visit first. They would get jealous if they weren't visited first. There was no dancing at the Id. That was only at the weddings. Also there was a chance to buy new clothes before the Id and we would wear them as we went visiting. That was exciting and important.'

Important foods eaten at Id in Palestine include: mansaf (lamb and rice), tamar hindi cordial, almond juice, fresh lemonade, kataif (sweet dish), and Ka'ak Al-Id (sweet bread).

A Palestinian describes memories of celebrations in Jerusalem:

'On the first day of the Id, in the morning, the young men go to the mosque to pray. In the streets there are boy-scout processions and music. After the prayers at the mosque, the men go to the cemetery to visit graves of family and then return home for breakfast. After breakfast, the men visit a dozen or so houses till lunch; in the afternoon the men stay home to receive visitors. Before sunset the women will visit the graves of their parents.

In the mosque the preacher explains about the significance of the Id: the value of visiting relatives, making peace with enemies, connecting with isolated community members, and helping the poor.

Games are played in the streets and public spaces, and in town swings and roundabouts may be set up. Children go from house to house singing with a candle and are given sweets.'

Turkey

'Throughout Ramadan we eat only freshly baked pita (flatbreads) for the fast-breaking meal. It is collected every day warm and fresh from the bakery just before the meal. On other months we eat other kinds of bread. During Ramadan the government organises free fairs and free food for the Ramadan nights and for the Id. The food is usually rice and meat and is distributed at the fairs free for poor people and also workers who are unable to travel home to break their fast. The fairs involve swings, roundabouts, puppets, storytellers and other entertainments.'

Sufi whirling dances are also performed in public during Ramadan evenings, involving slow graceful turning to the music. Sufis wear white gowns and hats for the ceremony, which is considered a kind of prayer.

On the first day of the Id, after morning prayers and breakfast, the young men go visiting relatives and the elders stay at home to receive guests. When children kiss the hand of an older relative and place it on their heads in a sign of respect, they are given money or sweets.

In Istanbul, 'Zakah' (the giving of alms) may be given directly to the poor; but in general it is mostly donated for the poor through the mosque. There is a tradition that a host gets spiritual credit for all the guests he entertains, so hosts are usually happy to have as many visitors as possible.

Uganda

Here are women's childhood memories of the Id in a Uganda village:

'Most children fasted for Ramadan after the age of eight, because children who fasted were rewarded with special food and presents, so the children did it as soon as they could. During Ramadan fasting was from 5am to 7pm. As Uganda is near the equator this does not change from year to year. Once the meal was finished in the evening, the Muslims would walk together to the mosque (there was a Muslim quarter in the village so all lived together and could walk together to the mosque). We would stay there for 3 – 4 hours, first praying and then listening to readings from the Qur'an and talks from the teachers. The men sit at the front and the women at the rear, divided by a curtain. All men attended. For women it was optional but many went too.

When I was young, the mosque was built of bamboo and mud, but now we have a modern building. On the floor of the mosque we would sit on reed mats woven by hand in the village, from the leaves of a local tree.

On the Id after Ramadan we would have a good meal. Typical foods were: green bananas, rice (this was a special treat in the village and eaten only on Id as it was imported and so expensive), chicken, sweet potatoes, cassava, English potatoes, and beef. On the Id day women would get up at 4am and work till 8am to get the food ready. At 8am there would be presents (mainly clothes and perhaps a little money) and then we would all go to the mosque.

On that day women would wear special clothes only for the Id – a loose white robe and headdress. It was the only time when we would cover our hair in the village. At the mosque we would pray and listen to religious stories and talks. We'd stay there till 1pm, then go home to eat and play. Sometimes we would go to the nearest town to the theatre as a special treat. There would be a little giving to the poor, but as the whole village was very poor, this was generally for close neighbours, usually some food or a piece of meat.'

Activity Ideas

+ Fasting for a day
+ Learning the white moon song
+ Designing and colouring a head/neck scarf
+ Designing and colouring a small tablecloth
+ Playing the hidden ring game
+ Making an Id pop-up card
+ Cooking Tawuq Coksi (sweet chicken)
+ Making Sherbatt Tamir Hindi (tamarind cordial)

Activity 1: fasting for a day

Note: A whole day's fast is not suitable for younger children. Children in Year 6 (age 10-11) could probably manage it.

Prepare yourself for fasting a few days before you intend to fast.

You will need to think about why you want to fast. It could be in thanks for God's mercies, to retreat from the routine of daily life, or to contemplate and meditate on the meaning of life and your part in it. Or it may be perhaps to discipline yourself to have self-control and resist temptations.

You may start your fast after the last meal of the day (that is the evening before the full day of fasting). Or you can follow the example of Muslim fasting by having a very early light meal an hour before dawn breaks (an extra early breakfast). Make sure you have a drink of water before you start your fast at dawn.

Make it your aim from the moment you start the fast that you will not be going to have anything to eat, drink or chew until sunset. To purify your soul, also work hard at being a positive person, not giving way to whims and moods. Do not lie, not even a white lie. Do not lose your temper. Do not talk about anyone negatively, and try not to indulge in any negative thoughts.

Do spend your time thinking about the world you live in. About your own life and conduct. About how to make yourself a better person. Do read some prayers and religious, spiritual, or moral texts and stories.

If you have chosen to fast while working, carry out your normal duties and work (if you have school, you should attend it). Fasting is not about stopping your duties; it is about disciplining your thoughts and deeds.

An hour before sunset, think about what you are going to eat at the break-fast time. Prepare a special meal. Traditionally, Muslims break their fast with three dates and a glass of plain yoghurt. You may wish to try something similar, perhaps with a glass of milk. Soup is the next traditional dish. Lentil soup is a favourite in many parts of the Middle East. Do not be tempted to taste the food you are preparing beforehand. Remember those who do not have the choice of food and when to eat it, the plight of the poor in our world.

Break your fast at sunset. There is no value in overdoing things. For Muslims, God will not reward fasters if they carry on fasting beyond the break-fast time. God is merciful and does not like his worshippers to become extreme, whether it is in their daily lives or in their spiritual lives. This is a very important point in Islam.

If you wish you may say a prayer of thanks for God's help in getting through the day without food and water. You may wish to spend the remainder of the evening in reading or praying, or discussing the experience of fasting and what it meant to you.

The Full Moon Song (Traditional)

O the full moon ro-ose o-ver us from the va-lley of Wa-da and we owe it to show gra-ti-tude where the call is to All-ah Oh- you who were rai-sed a-mongst us with a call to be o-beyed; you have brought our ci-ty no-ble-ness wel-come best cal-ler to God's way O the ...

Activity 2: learning the white moon song

O the full moon rose over us
From the valley of Wada
And we owe it to show gratitude
Where the call is to Allah

O you who were raised amongst us
Coming with a word to be obeyed
You have brought our city nobility
Welcome best caller to God's way

Activity 3: designing and colouring a head/neck scarf

This activity could also be adjusted to make a tablecloth design. You may choose to make your own design by using the sample patterns section at the end of this book, or use the scarf design given here.

Materials:
90cm x 90cm washable textile, thin and soft cotton or synthetic fabric, preferably light in colour (easier to draw the pattern on). Avoid stretchy fabrics as they are difficult to control in hand painting.

Water-based textile paints (not dyes), applied with brushes, and suitable for the type of fabric you have chosen.

Water-based textile liners, suitable for drawing
 lines on cloth. They come in paste tubes
 that are easy to use.
Brushes, paper tissues, and a bowl of water
 for cleaning them
Carbon paper
Ballpoint pen, pencil, ruler, scissors, etc.
Pins, needle, thread for hemming the edges
 of the scarf
Sellotape
Plain white paper (to be used as a wrist rest)

Method:

1 Cut the cloth to the exact size you need
 (90cm x 90cm adult size, or 70cm x 70cm
 for a child).

2 Hem the square all round and iron the
 edges. You may wish to do the hemming
 using a sewing machine, or stitch it by
 hand. Both are good opportunities to
 teach children both techniques.

3 Enlarge the scarf design on a
 photocopying machine, or make your own
 design. In both cases, the size needs to fit
 the textile.

4 Cover the work surface with plastic
 sheeting, sticking it securely to the surface
 with sellotape.

5 Spread out the textile on the plastic
 sheeting and fix down, from the edges
 only, using the sellotape. Make sure the
 fabric is firmly spread and has no wrinkles.

6 Using the carbon paper, transfer the design onto the textile: place the carbon paper on the textile, sandwiched between it and the design. Secure the carbon paper and the design with sellotape. Use a ballpoint pen to trace the design, pressing firmly.

7 After tracing the pattern, remove the sheet of paper and the carbon paper. You are now ready to colour.

8 Have your textile colours, brushes, bowl of water, and the tissues nearby, but not on the textile. Test out the colours you want to use on a scrap of textile.

9 Colour in. Make sure to colour the farthest parts first, so that you do not risk smudging. Use the plain white paper to support the hand that holds the brush at the wrist and avoid damaging the traced patterns on the fabric.

10 When you have finished colouring, leave to dry for at least 24 hours, before removing from the table.

11 Using a hot iron, and an ironing cloth, iron the scarf to fix down the paint permanently. Be careful not to let the iron directly touch the paint.

12 The scarf is now complete and ready for wearing.

Activity 4: designing and colouring a small tablecloth

Materials:

Thick, washable, light-coloured
cotton fabric (120cm x
40cm). You may wish to alter
the dimensions to suit a
specific table you have

Water-based textile colours
suitable for cottons (see scarf
activity for more information)

Colouring and craft tools (See
scarf activity for more
information)

Method:

1 Cut the textile to size.
2 Fray the two narrow edges by
removing the horizontal
threads carefully, until the
fringe is 3cm deep.
3 Hem the two long edges and
stick appropriately.
4 Follow the instructions for
making the headscarf when
transferring the design and
colouring in the tablecloth.

Design for small Table-Cloth

Activity 5: playing the hidden ring game

This is a concentration game that needs wit and patience. It is a very good game for a class or a large group of people. It works best when there are more than six people in each team. The tradition of using a ring in this game is of no religious meaning or significance, just fun after a long day of fasting.

How to play it:

1 You need a ring, preferably a small one.
2 Decide how many rounds you intend to play. We recommend no less than four rounds to give a fair chance to both sides. If you have more rounds, make sure that they are an even number to ensure equal opportunities.
3 The group is divided into two teams (A&B) and two leaders (A&B). It is not too important for the two teams to be exactly equal in number, as long as they are roughly so.
4 Each team sits in rows opposite each other.

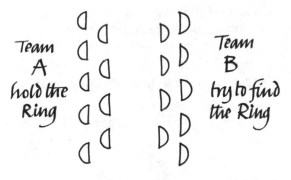

Team A hold the Ring

Team B try to find the Ring

5 Make sure that the back rows are higher than the front, as it is crucial that all fists are held up and visible to the opposing team.
6 One member is elected to monitor the game and keep score.
7 Each team identifies a leader, who stands by his group. He (leader A) is also the bearer of the ring.

The Ring-Bearer holds the Ring in between both his hands

8 When all are seated, a coin is tossed to see which team starts the game by hiding the ring amongst its members.
9 The 'ring bearer', leader A, while turning his back to his opponents, starts to go through his team line by line, pretending to position the ring in each pair of hands. The ring bearer holds the ring between his closed hands (with outstretched fingers).
10 Each team A member receives the imaginary or real ring by holding his hands together in a similar fashion, but slightly open (like a book) so that the ring bearer can slide his hands though them, depositing the ring if he chooses to do so.
11 Whether the ring is deposited or not, and with whom, must be known to no one except the ring bearer and the person who is given it.

Team-Member's hands

12 Each team member receiving the leader's hands – whether the ring is left with him or not – must quickly close his fists, pretending that he may have the ring in one of his fists. He then keeps his two fists closed in front of his chest, and will not open them until asked to by the opposite side.

Team Member's hands

Leader's hands

13 Once the leader has slid his hands through the hands of all his team, he stands aside to watch the game. He must deposit the ring with someone before he finishes. He cannot choose to keep the ring in his own hands.

The team player must close his fists quickly – pretending that he may have the Ring in one of them

14 Now the opposite team B and its leader B, 'the ring finder', are invited to try and find the ring. The ring finder is free to consult with his team on their observations.

15 The ring finder starts examining the closed fists lined in front of him. He must not touch any of them.

16 The ring finder then chooses a fist where he thinks the ring is **not** held, and the player chosen must open his fist. If the ring is there then the ring finder's team has lost and a new round begins. If the fist is empty then he may choose another fist which he thinks is empty, and so on (i.e. one by one fists are eliminated and the number of places where the ring might be is narrowed down).

17 If at any stage of the game the ring finder feels confident that he now knows in which fist the ring is held, he can point to it and ask for the ring to be handed over from this fist.

18 If the ring is correctly found the round is over and the ring finder's team B get one point for this round.

19 If the ring turns out not to be in the hand chosen by the ring finder, the round is also over, and team A get a point.

20 Everyone in the team with the ring must control their facial expressions and body language, and not give anything away.

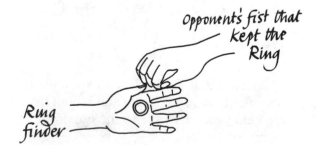

Opponent's fist that kept the Ring

Ring finder

They must also resist any intimidation or off-guard questions from their opponents. They must not open their fists for any reason (not even to blow their noses!)

21 The next round starts by passing the ring to team B to hide, and for team A to find. The ultimate winner will be the team that gets the highest number of points.

22 The losing team has to treat all the participants and audience to a tray of Baklava or other sweet dishes.

Activity 6: *making an Id pop-up card*

Materials:
Card of any colour for the base
White card for the pop-up images
Colouring pens, pencils, or pastels
Pencil, ruler, scissors
Carbon paper
Glue

Method:
1 Fold one sheet of the coloured card to form the base (the main body of the card).
2 Copy the designs of the angels with their fixing tabs onto the white card, and colour them in.
3 Cut them out with their tabs.
4 Fold along the dotted lines, so that the angels close on themselves.
5 Open the base card flat on to the table.
6 Glue down the angels:
  a the top angel first.
  b fold him inwards.
  c glue the tabs.
  d fix side, at an angle, on the base card, making sure that the bottom corner of the fold lines up with the centre fold of the base card.
  e fold back the other glued tab, and fold over it the other side of the base card.
  f press down well so that the second tab is fixed on to the other side of the card.
  When you open the card the angel should rise to stand upright.
7 Do the same thing as above to the two other angels, fixing them below the top angel at a reasonable distance so that

when you open the card you have two rows of angels.

8 Decorate the front of the card using the Id greeting 'Id Said' in Arabic calligraphy and its English equivalent 'Happy Festival'.

Activity 7: *cooking Tawuq Coksi (sweet chicken)*

This Turkish sweet dish combines chicken and milk.

Ingredients:
5 cups milk (full-fat preferred, but semi-skimmed would do)
3 tablespoons rice flour
1 chicken breast
3/4 cup sugar
1 teaspoon cinnamon powder

Method:
1 Boil the chicken breasts until tender.
2 Soak the cooked breasts in cold water for 8 hours.
3 Remove from the water and dry.
4 Using your fingers shred the breast fibres as finely as you can (the finer the better).
5 Mix the milk and sugar in a pot, and place on the stove until the sugar is fully dissolved. Remove from the stove.
6 Add the shredded chicken breast to the milk and sugar mixture, and return to the stove, on medium heat. Mix and stir for at least 10 minutes, until the chicken is well blended into the milk and sugar mixture.
7 Separately, mix the rice flour with a little bit of water.
8 Add the rice flour mixture to the milk and chicken, continuing to stir, while still on the stove, for a good while and until the mixture thickens well.
9 Remove from the heat and serve, decorating the surface of the dish with the cinnamon powder; serve hot.

Make an Id Pop-up Card

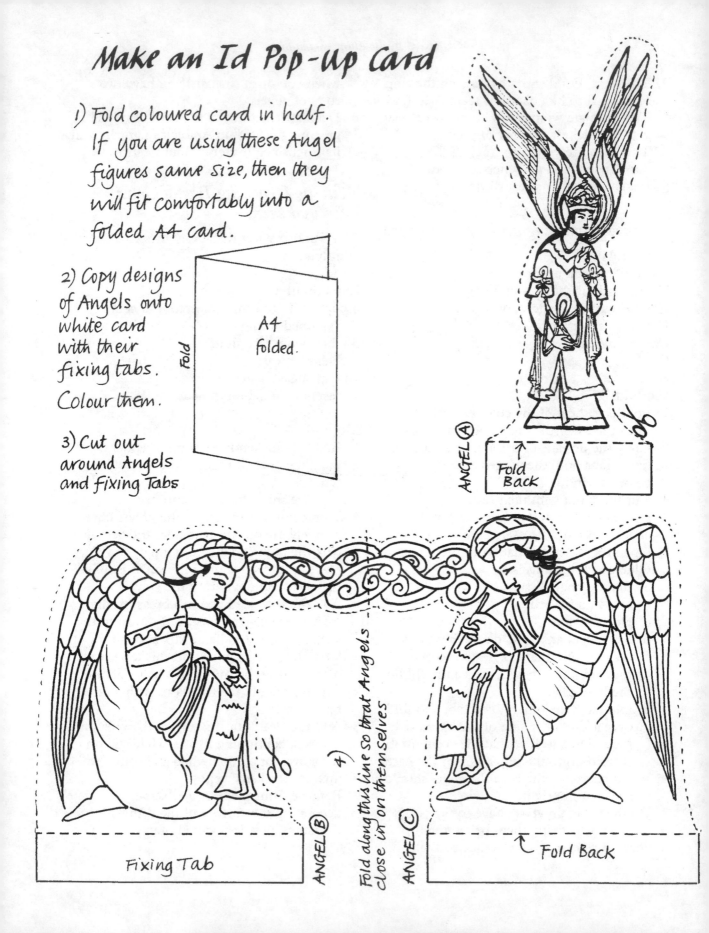

1) Fold coloured card in half. If you are using these Angel figures same size, then they will fit comfortably into a folded A4 card.

A4 folded.

Fold

2) Copy designs of Angels onto white card with their fixing tabs.

Colour them.

3) Cut out around Angels and Fixing Tabs

ANGEL A

Fold Back

ANGEL B

Fixing Tab

4) Fold along this line so that Angels close in on themselves

ANGEL C

Fold Back

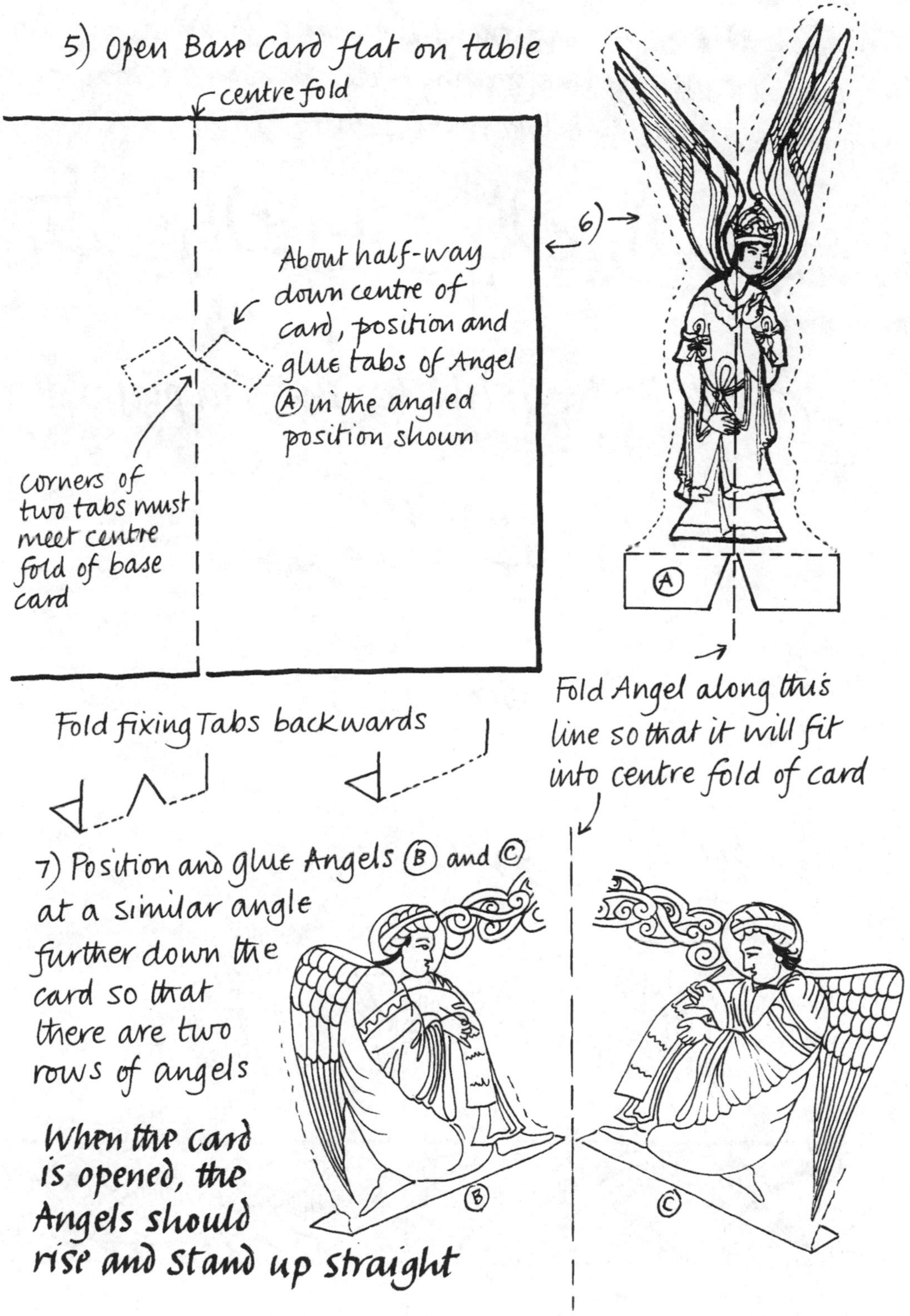

5) Open Base Card flat on table

centre fold

About half-way down centre of card, position and glue tabs of Angel Ⓐ in the angled position shown

corners of two tabs must meet centre fold of base card

6) →

Fold Angel along this line so that it will fit into centre fold of card

Fold fixing Tabs backwards

7) Position and glue Angels Ⓑ and Ⓒ at a similar angle further down the card so that there are two rows of angels

When the card is opened, the Angels should rise and stand up straight

155

8) Decorate the front of the card with an appropriate message and greeting. You can copy the Arabic greetings below or just write 'Happy Id'!

مع اطيب التمنيات بالعيدالسعيد

With Best Wishes for the Happy Id ⌐

عيد مبارك

Blessed Id ⌐

عيد سعيد

Activity 8: making Sherbatt Tamir Hindi (tamarind cordial)

This drink is popular in many Middle Eastern countries. This recipe is from Palestine.

Ingredients:

1/2 kg red tamarind, or 1 cup of concentrated tamarind paste
12 cups water
3/4 cup lemon juice
3 kg white sugar

Method:

1 Pick (or buy) red tamarind, wash and cut into small pieces.
2 Soak for 12 hours in cold water.
3 Put the soaked tamarind with its water in a pot and heat, boiling it for 5 minutes.
4 Drain the tamarind in a fine sieve.
5 Measure out the sieved juice, with the aim of making 12 cups of the cordial. Make up the additional quantity needed with plain water, which should then be used to dissolve the sugar.
6 Dissolve the sugar in the plain water measured to make up the difference. Put on low heat to help the process. Remove any froth that accumulates on the surface of the liquid. Heat until the mixture thickens.
7 Add the tamarind juice to the water and sugar, and leave on the stove for five minutes before adding the lemon juice. Boil for a further five minutes.
8 Sieve the cordial, leave to cool, and then bottle.

Stories of Generosity

During the period when the Prophet lived in Madinah, the first Muslim community was established. Muhammad provided detailed teachings on how a Muslim community should live and be organised. One of the important principles he taught was the duty of generosity to others in the community, and in particular the poor, neighbours and family members. Ramadan and the two feasts are times when Muslims practise generosity towards family and the poor. The stories in this section explore this theme from different points of view.

Juha Saves the Miser

This tale, in one form or another, is told throughout the Islamic world. This particular version comes from Iran.

In Juha's village there was an old miser who never gave anything to anyone, not even to the poor during Ramadan. Once the miser fell into the village pond. It was deep and the miser could not swim. Villagers went down to the pond edge and called out: 'Give us your hand! Give us your hand!' But the miser refused to grab their outstretched hands.

It happened that Juha was passing by. He saw what was happening and told the villagers to stand back. He held out his hand and called out 'Take my hand! Take my hand!' and the miser immediately grabbed hold of Juha's hand and was dragged to safety.

A Generous Curse

A holy man was walking by the side of a dusty road with his student. They had been walking all day and were thirsty and tired when a carriage drawn by six horses came speeding along the road. As it approached the driver shouted down to them:

'Get out of the way! Get out of the way you old fool.'

The holy man and his student tried to get out of the way but they were too slow and the speeding carriage knocked them off the road and into the ditch.

The holy man stood up and shook his fist at the carriage:

'May all your needs be satisfied!' he shouted as the carriage disappeared around the next bend.

The student was puzzled. 'Teacher, why did you shout that?' he asked.

The holy man smiled. 'Do you think if all his needs were satisfied he would have knocked us into the ditch?'

A Generous Gift

Turkmenistan is famous for its hospitality and its fine horses. In a particular village there was a man with a fine horse which his neighbour wanted to buy. Time and again the neighbour visited. It is the custom in Turkmenistan that before a visitor discusses business he should share a meal with his host, and so on each visit the neighbour ate a meal before offering to buy the horse. Time and time again the owner refused.

Then the owner fell on hard times, and became very poor until the only thing he had left was his fine horse. When his neighbour visited, they sat down together and ate a meal together before the neighbour asked if he could now buy the horse.

'I'm afraid you cannot,' replied the owner. 'The meat in this food we are eating is the meat from my horse. It would be shameful not to offer meat to a visitor, and so I had to kill it.'

Abu Kassim's Boots

This story is very well known throughout the Arab world. It can be found in the popular 'One Thousand and One Nights', which brought tales like Aladdin and Sinbad to the West. While the story is set in Iraq, the origin of the tale is not known.

Once, in the city of Baghdad, there was a merchant called Abu Kassim. Abu Kassim was a hard worker. Every day he was the first to come into the market and the last to leave. He always bought at the lowest possible price and sold at the highest, and in this way he became very rich. Indeed some said he was the richest merchant in the market.

But Abu Kassim did not look like the richest merchant in the market. His robe was frayed and torn, and his headscarf was so old it had lost all its colour after years of bleaching in the sun. But if his robe and headscarf looked old, that was nothing compared with his boots. Abu Kassim had worn the same pair of boots for 20 years. Every time there was a hole in the shoe, Abu Kassim got a leather patch put over it. And when the patch got a hole in it he patched the patch. In this way the boots got bigger and bigger, heavier and heavier, but Abu Kassim would not throw them away.

'Waste not, want not; look after the pennies and the pounds will take care of themselves,' were his watchwords. He never bought anything for himself or his family unless he absolutely had to. His children ate the plainest of foods, wore old, patched clothes, and lived in a tiny house with almost no furniture.

Abu Kassim was a mean old miser. He never gave to charity. In Ramadan, when all Muslims were expected to give to the poor, Abu Kassim never did, always finding some excuse or other. He never helped his neighbours or his friends when they were in need. He just saved up the money he made and kept it in a box in his house.

Now while all merchants in Baghdad wanted to make money, it was also expected that those who were rich had a duty to help those who were poor. The richer the man, the greater was his duty to use his wealth wisely. For this reason, the merchants in the market felt sorry for Abu Kassim. Many tried to give him advice, but he never took it. In the end he became something of a joke in the market.

If someone was hanging on to something they should get rid of, like an old shirt or robe, then people would say 'That's like the boots of Abu Kassim!' If someone had a bad habit that they couldn't get rid of, then it would also be compared to Abu Kassim's boots. With time, as Abu Kassim's boots grew bigger and bigger, with more and more patches added, so they became more and more famous.

Our story begins with Abu Kassim in a very good mood. That day he had bought two items at a very low price: a large barrel of perfume and a case of tiny perfume bottles. His plan was to fill the bottles with perfume and sell them at a very high price and so make a good profit.

Abu Kassim was in such a good mood he decided to do something he only did once a

year. He decided to have a bath. In those days people didn't have baths in their homes. When they wanted a bath they went to the public baths where they could soak and wash themselves.

That day Abu Kassim walked down to the public baths in his heavy old boots. He paid the copper coin needed to enter and went to his changing cubicle. As he was walking to the cubicle another merchant saw him plodding along – his boots were so heavy with all those patches that it took a real effort to lift up his foot, so he tended to slide the boots along the ground instead. The merchant decided to give Abu Kassim a little advice.

'Abu Kassim,' he called out. 'Peace to you and glory to God. Forgive me for intruding, but as your neighbour in the market I feel it is my duty to give you some advice. Abu Kassim, you should get some new boots. The ones you wear are ridiculous. Everyone laughs at them and you can't even walk properly in them. Get some new ones, my friend, and you'll feel better.'

Abu Kassim frowned at the merchant. 'My friend,' he grumbled, 'I would thank you to mind your own business and not mine. These boots have got a good few miles in them yet and I won't be changing them. People like you who laugh and gossip behind my back: I know about you all! I know that you are jealous because your miserable little businesses are not doing as well as mine. That is because you don't work hard and you waste money on useless things. I'll thank you to mind your own business and leave me alone!'

While Abu Kassim plodded off to his cubicle and started to undress for his bath, the merchant was furious. How impolite! How rude of him! The merchant decided to play a trick on Abu Kassim and teach him a lesson.

He noticed that the changing cubicle next to Abu Kassim was being used by the chief judge of the town, the Qadi. Now that day the Qadi had bought himself some brand new soft leather shoes, which he had left in the cubicle with his other clothes while he took his bath. The merchant waited until Abu Kassim had gone to his bath, and then he switched over the shoes in the cubicles. Abu Kassim's boots went into the judge's cubicle and the judge's new shoes went into Abu Kassim's cubicle.

Abu Kassim didn't stay long in his bath as he wanted to get back to work. When he returned to his changing cubicle, he saw the new shoes on the floor and thought 'How kind! Someone has seen my old shoes and made me a present of some new ones! How kind. I knew it would be a waste of money to buy some new ones. Look, now I've got some new ones for nothing!'

Abu Kassim got dressed and went skipping off down the road, admiring his soft leather shoes, happy at how light his feet felt without the heavy old things he used to wear.

A while later the Qadi got back from his bath and saw that his new shoes were missing and a dirty old pair of boots was there in his place. He recognised them immediately and ordered Abu Kassim to be arrested and brought to his court. Soldiers went to Abu Kassim's shop, arrested him and dragged him in front of the Qadi.

'Abu Kassim,' thundered the judge. 'You have stolen my shoes. How dare you!'

'But your honour…it is a mistake …I didn't mean it…I didn't know they were yours…I am innocent!'

'Do you take me for a fool? How could you mistake my new shoes for your old boots. No, my friend, you are guilty and must be punished. Pay a fine of 500 dinars or go to jail. Your choice!'

Abu Kassim didn't want to go to jail and so he had to pay. When he had handed over the money, he set off for home barefoot, holding his old boots by their laces. He was in such a rotten mood he started shouting at the boots.

'How could you do this to me! After all the years I've looked after you, taken care of you, patched you, not thrown you away, you repay me like this! I could have bought 500 new pairs of shoes with the fine I just paid because of you! Well that's it. I've had enough. Good-bye boots.'

Abu Kassim was walking past the river that ran through the centre of Baghdad. He swung the boots around his head and flung them out into the middle of the river.

'Good riddance to bad rubbish!' he muttered and walked off home. There he started filling the bottles with perfume.

'When I sell these, I will make more than 5000 dinars profit,' he thought, and the thought cheered him up.

A while later a fisherman was pulling in his net in that same river, a little downstream from where Abu Kassim had thrown away his boots. As he pulled in his net he felt something quite heavy.

'Maybe a big fish,' he thought, and imagined selling the fish and what he would buy with the money from the sale. But when the net was heaved onto the shore, there were only two smelly old boots. What was worse, the nails from the boots had ripped holes into the net so that the fisherman would have to spend at least a day mending it before he could go fishing again. The fisherman was furious. Then he recognised the boots, the famous boots of Abu Kassim. He was so cross he marched over to Abu Kassim's house, threw the boots through his open window, and went away.

Now it happened that behind the window was Abu Kassim's storeroom where he kept all his merchandise. The two boots sailed through the window and crashed into the shelf holding all of those tiny bottles, now filled with expensive perfume. The shelf fell over and all the bottles broke on the floor. Abu Kassim heard a crash, and when he rushed into the room he saw his bottles all smashed in a puddle of perfume. There in the centre of the puddle were his old boots!

'What are you doing here?' he shouted at the boots. 'And why are you doing this to me? First you cost me 500 dinars, and now this. I have lost 5000 dinars because of you! I don't want to see you and your ugly old patches. I'll… I'll… I'll bury you in the garden… that'll fix you!'

Abu Kassim took the boots and a spade and went into his garden. He started to dig a deep hole where he would get rid of those boots. As he dug he muttered curses under his breath at his boots.

Now it happened that there was a law in the city forbidding digging for treasure without permission. As Abu Kassim was digging and muttering in his garden, two soldiers passed by. They watched him for a while, then one of them called out,

'What are you doing there? Why are you digging? Don't you know it's forbidden to dig for treasure? Explain yourself man!'

Abu Kassim looked up. 'I'm burying my boots,' he said angrily and went back to his digging.

'Do you think we are fools?' said the soldier. 'Nobody buries their boots. That is not a good reason for digging a hole. You are digging for treasure and that's against the law. I'm afraid you'll have to come with us.'

So Abu Kassim and his boots were taken to the Qadi's court.

'You again!' roared the Qadi when he saw Abu Kassim. 'First you steal my shoes, and now this. Looking for treasure without permission is a serious offence.'

'But I wasn't looking for treasure,' whined Abu Kassim. 'I was burying my boots.'

'Surely you can think of a better excuse than that,' growled the Qadi. 'Pay a fine of 50,000 dinars or go to jail. It's your choice.'

Well Abu Kassim didn't want to go to jail, so he had to go home and take a small sack of gold coins out of his savings box and give it to the Qadi. On his way back from the court he started cursing his boots again.

'50,000 dinars! 50,000 dinars! How could you do this to me, you rotten boots? It took me a whole year to earn that and now it's gone just because of you. And you are worth not even a dinar. After all I did for you, over the years, this is how you repay me. Well I never want to see you again. Goodbye boots!'

At this moment Abu Kassim was walking past an open sewage channel which carried wastewater away from the houses. Abu Kassim dropped the boots in the channel and watched as they floated away down the channel until they were out of sight.

'That's the last I'll have to see of you!' he said to himself.

The boots floated down the channel for a while, until the channel fed into a sewer pipe. The boots were sucked down the pipe, and travelled with the current for a while, until the pipe began to get narrower and narrower.

Finally the boots got stuck in the pipe, blocking it and preventing sewage flowing past. The pipe filled up with sewage, and soon sewage was flooding all over the city, through the streets and into the houses.

The city engineers were called to fix the blockage. They dug and they poked and they probed until finally, they found the source of the blockage. Abu Kassim's boots!

Abu Kassim was dragged in front of the Qadi and ordered to pay 500,000 dinars for the clean-up of the city. He had to pay, or face execution, and so he paid, using all the savings he had built up over twenty years as a trader. He left the court still carrying his boots, and took them home.

'I know what I'll do', he thought, 'I'll burn these terrible boots. I'll burn them in the garden.' But the boots were still wet from the sewage, so he had to dry them out first. Abu Kassim put the boots on his roof to dry in the sun.

A while later a little puppy came scampering up onto the roof and started to play with the boots. He bit into one, he pounced on the other, biting and pouncing, pouncing and biting until one of the boots was knocked off the roof. The boot fell down towards the street, onto the head of a young woman who happened to be passing by. She was pregnant with her first child, and when the boot hit her on the head it gave her such a shock that she miscarried, losing the baby.

Her family was furious and complained to the Qadi, who summoned Abu Kassim to the court.

'Abu Kassim, I am getting tired of seeing your face,' thundered the Qadi. 'You must pay for this crime'.

'But it wasn't me,' wailed Abu Kassim, 'It was my boots, they did it, not me!' 'You are responsible for those boots,' replied the judge, 'and you must pay compensation for what happened.'

'Your honour, I agree. I agree to pay compensation, but on one condition. Please can a paper be drawn up by this court stating that whatever these boots do from now on it is not my fault. I disown these boots. They are not mine. I do not want them!'

The judge smiled and agreed. The paper was drawn up and Abu Kassim paid compensation to the family, giving them the last of his possessions. He left the court penniless but wiser, happy that he had finally got rid of his hated boots.

When his business picked up again he was a changed man. He gave to the poor during Ramadan, helped his neighbours, and made sure his children had good food and proper clothes. Once every year he bought himself a brand new pair of shoes!

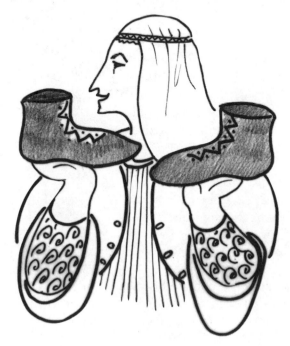

163

Chapter 7

HOMECOMING

The first house of worship appointed for men was that at [Makkah]; full of blessing and of guidance for all creation. In it are signs manifest: the station of Abraham; whoever enters it attains security. Pilgrimage thereto is a duty men owe to God, for those who can afford the journey.

The Qur'an: *Surat Al-Imran*

The Return to Makkah and the Prophet's Death

In previous chapters we read how, in the holy city of Makkah, Muhammad began to preach God's message. He taught the worship of one God, and for this he was persecuted by pagan tribal chiefs. Finally, when his life was in danger, God instructed him to leave Makkah. Muhammad travelled to the town of Madinah where he created the first Islamic community.

Eight years after Muhammad had moved from Makkah to Madinah, Islam was rapidly growing in strength. Muhammad had gathered a large body of followers in Madinah and elsewhere, and a strong army willing to fight for him. Over that period there had been a series of clashes between tribes from Makkah and Madinah. Time and again, peace treaties were made, but the Makkah tribes had repeatedly broken their agreements with Muhammad.

Eventually the Prophet decided to conquer Makkah, in order to protect it for Muslim worship. He marched on Makkah with an army of 10,000 warriors, an army so strong that the people of Makkah surrendered with hardly a drop of blood spilled.

As soon as Muhammad entered the city his first act was to forgive all those who had stood against him. In those days conquering armies often took revenge against the people they had conquered, and so Muhammad's mercy won him great respect from the people he had conquered. Before long most of the people in the city had voluntarily accepted Islam.

Next the Prophet went to the House of God, which was surrounded by hundreds of stone statues that were worshipped as gods. Muhammad ordered that all of these statues be smashed and removed, erasing symbols of false gods from the holy place. From that day onwards, twenty-one years after his first revelation, the House of God was re-dedicated to the worship of the one God.

After the conquest of Makkah, the Prophet returned to his home in Madinah. But two years later he performed a special pilgrimage to Makkah, a spiritual journey known as the Hajj. This journey became the fifth and last core teaching (pillar) of Islam. All Muslims are required, if they are able, to make the sacred journey to Makkah at least once in their lifetime.

Before Muhammad there had already been a tradition of making a pilgrimage to Makkah, but with this instruction the duty of Hajj became the fifth and final core teaching of the Muslim faith.

The story of Abraham and Ishmael

During the Hajj, and the Festival of Sacrifice which follows, Muslims reflect on the following story (also see Chapter 1).

Once an angel appeared before Abraham, and told him that he should sacrifice his own son. This was a terrible thing for a father to do, but Abraham believed in obeying God's will and so was bound to carry out the order.

When Abraham told Ishmael what the angel had said, the boy showed great courage and faith, replying that if God had ordered this then he should do it without hesitation.

'Don't be afraid,' he said. 'With God's help I shall be brave.'

Abraham took his son to a quiet place, and there drew his knife, preparing to kill the boy. But at that moment he heard a voice, saying that he had proved his obedience and that he should not now kill his son, but rather a ram instead. In this way Ishmael was saved and Abraham understood that God had been testing his faith and obedience.

Death of the Prophet

A few months after completing the Hajj, at the age of 63, the Prophet died. He left behind two sources of inspiration for his followers: his words and his deeds. His divinely inspired words are recorded in the holy Qur'an, the sacred book for all Muslims.

The spread of Islam

Within 100 years of Muhammad's death, Muslim Arab armies had conquered an enormous empire stretching from Spain in the West to India in the East. While the aim of the armies was to spread the word of Islam, the Arabs did not force their subjects to become Muslims. They were still free to practise their own religion, but had to pay a special tax to their rulers. Over time, more and more people in the conquered areas became Muslims. Today Muslims live in countries throughout the world. Countries with a Muslim majority in their population are found in sub-Saharan Africa, Central Europe and Eastern Asia as well as the Arab world.

Countries with a Majority of Muslims in the Population

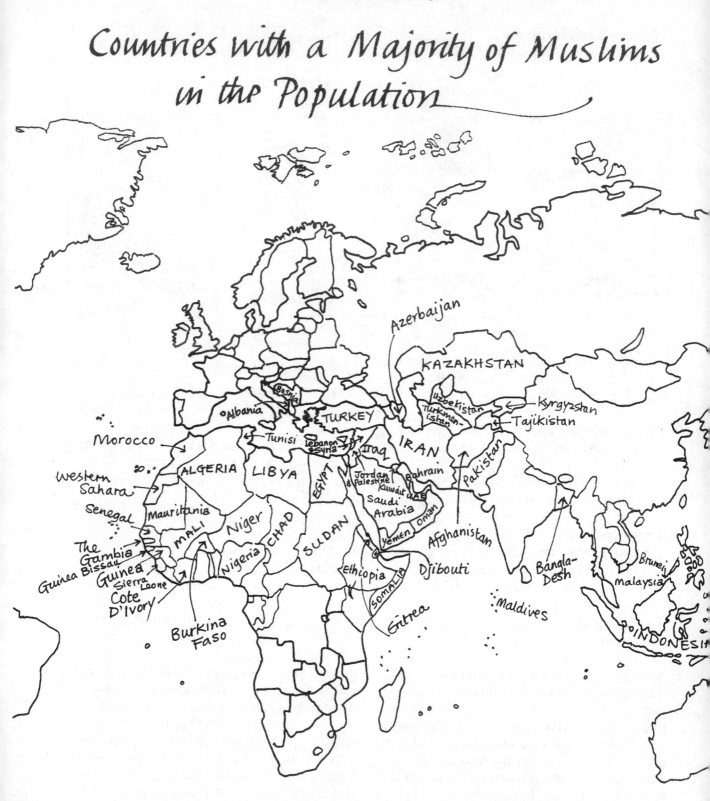

Azerbaijan

KAZAKHSTAN

Bosnia

Albania

TURKEY

Uzbekistan
Turk-men-
istan

Kyrgyzstan

Tajikistan

Morocco

Tunisi

Lebanon
Syria

Iraq

IRAN

Western
Sahara

ALGERIA

LIBYA

EGYPT

Jordan
& Palestine

Bahrain

Kuwait
UAE

Pakistan

Senegal

Mauritania

Saudi
Arabia

Afghanistan

Guinea
Bissau

The
Gambia

MALI

Niger

CHAD

SUDAN

Yemen

Oman

Bangla-
Desh

Guinea

Sierra
Leone

Nigeria

Brunei

malaysia

Cote
D'Ivory

Ethiopia

Djibouti

SOMALIA

Maldives

INDONESIA

Burkina
Faso

Eritrea

Countries with a majority of Muslims in the population

Afghanistan	Guinea-Bissau	Pakistan
Albania	Indonesia	Palestine
Algeria	Iran	Qatar
Azerbaijan	Iraq	Saudi Arabia
Bahrain	Jordan	Senegal
Bangladesh	Kazakhstan	Sierra Leone
Bosnia and Herzegovina	Kyrgyzstan	Somalia
Brunei	Kuwait	Sudan
Burkina Faso	Lebanon	Syria
Chad	Libya	Tajikistan
Comoros	Malaysia	Tunisia
Cote d'Ivory	Maldives	Turkey
Djibouti	Mali	Turkmenistan
Egypt	Mauritania	United Arab Emirates
Eritrea	Morocco	Uzbekistan
Ethiopia	Niger	Western Sahara
The Gambia	Nigeria	Yemen
Guinea	Oman	

The Pilgrimage

What is the pilgrimage to Makkah?

Most religions have special, sacred places that have important meaning for their faith, with traditions of making journeys there for prayer and reflection. Such a journey is a pilgrimage; those who make the journey are pilgrims.

The pilgrimage to Makkah is known as the Hajj, when pilgrims visit the House of God (Ka'bah), to perform specific rituals of worship dedicated to God, and in remembrance of the prophets Abraham and Muhammad.

Those who have made the pilgrimage may be addressed with the title Hajj (or Hajji for women) as a sign of respect for their accomplishment. For example, a man called Mustapha would be called 'Hajj Mustapha'.

Why go on a pilgrimage?

Pilgrimage is a form of worship, like saying prayers, reading the holy scriptures, and fasting. The House of God was originally built by Abraham (see Chapter 1), the first house built specifically for the worship of God. All Muslims, as we have heard, are required to visit this house at least once in their lifetime if they are able.

The pilgrimage involves sacrificing the company of family and friends, giving up the comforts of home, travelling away from one's homeland, giving up traditional dress, make-up and jewellery, and bearing the financial costs of the trip. A pilgrim must put aside his normal daily life, including his social status and wealth.

Many pilgrims experience a deep sense of relationship with God during their journey.

When does the pilgrimage take place?

The Hajj takes place at a specific time each year, in the month of Dhul Hijjah, the twelfth month in the Islamic Calendar (see Chapter 5). Muslims arrive in Makkah before the eighth day of the month, when six days of ceremonies begin.

How do people go on pilgrimage?

Until the second half of the 20th century, travelling to Makkah from other countries involved a long and difficult journey by land and sea. Pilgrims travelled from as far as Malaysia and Mongolia, some taking more than a year to complete their journey.

The old caravan routes through Asia and the Middle East were used not only for trade, but also by pilgrims. Camels were usually used for the long trip across the desert. Pilgrims from North Africa travelled overland to the Red Sea and then by boat to Arabia.

Most pilgrims travelled in groups. There were a few stations on the borders of the desert where pilgrims could join up with a group of travellers known as 'caravans'. Group travel was, and still is the norm. It was very rare to see individuals travelling on their own. The caravans which people joined left from specific stations on the borders of the Arabian Peninsula.

Modern transport, buses and aeroplanes have now taken over from camels and boats, and around three million Muslims go on the pilgrimage each year.

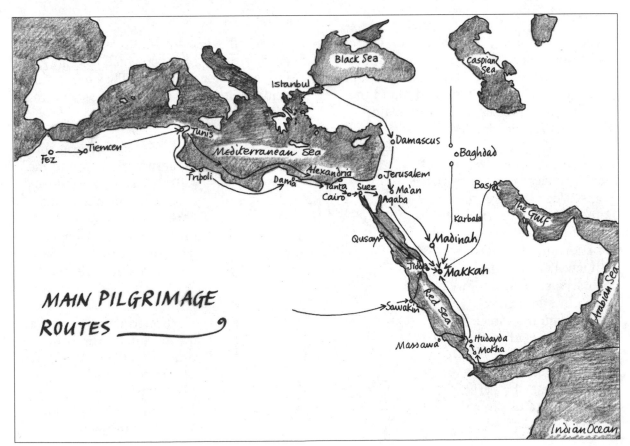

MAIN PILGRIMAGE ROUTES _____

What does a pilgrim do once he/she arrives in Makkah?

The clothes

Every pilgrim brings special clothes for the Hajj ceremonies, known as 'Ihram' clothes. These consist of two pieces of seamless, plain white cloth. These are wrapped round the body for male pilgrims; and very plainly sewn together for females.

The white cloth is a symbol of the pilgrim's search for spiritual purity. While wearing these clothes the pilgrim enters a state of purity: he/she should not adorn himself/herself with jewellery or other decorations, involve himself/ herself in argument or dispute, commit violence or have sexual relations.

As all pilgrims wear the same clothes, all external symbols of status are gone.

Visiting the House of God

Pilgrims, all dressed in white, walk to the main mosque in Makkah which has the House of God at its centre. They enter the mosque reciting prayers and passages from the Qur'an.

Once in the main central court, the pilgrims circle round the Ka'bah seven times, anti-clockwise, starting at the corner that contains the black stone (see Chapter 1). This ritual expresses the common aim of all pilgrims to worship God.

Next pilgrims go to pray at the Station of Abraham, situated in the central court next to the Ka'bah. In the prayer they honour Abraham's role in building the House of God.

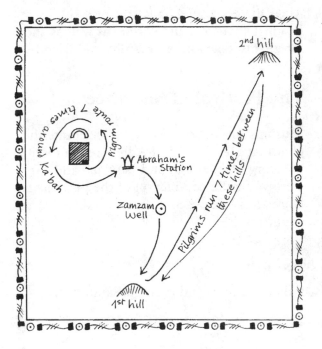

Mina and Arafat

When the rituals in Makkah are complete, many of the pilgrims spend a day in Mina, a town half way between Makkah and the plain of Arafat, where all are due to gather on the 9th day of Dhul Hijjah. At Mina, pilgrims spend the day in prayer and contemplation, preparing themselves for the coming gathering at Arafat.

On the morning of the 9th day of Dhul Hijjah all pilgrims meet on the Plain of Arafat, following in the footsteps of Muhammad on his final pilgrimage many years before. When the sun crosses the highest point in the sky, a sermon is preached, followed by midday and afternoon prayers. The words of God echo in the minds of the faithful, affirming they are all equal before God.

Next pilgrims go to drink from the waters of the well 'Zamzam', the miraculous spring which once saved the lives of Abraham's wife and child (see Chapter 1).

After this pilgrims cross to two small hills either side of the Ka'bah. Pilgrims walk and run backwards and forwards between these two hills seven times, just as Abraham's wife had done many years before.

The next day pilgrims arrive back in Mina, where they perform a stone-throwing ritual, which the Prophet himself was said to have performed on his pilgrimage.

Pilgrims throw stones at three white pillars. These represent the temptation to disobey God's commands. The pillars are said to be at the place where Satan tempted Abraham to disobey God's command to sacrifice his son.

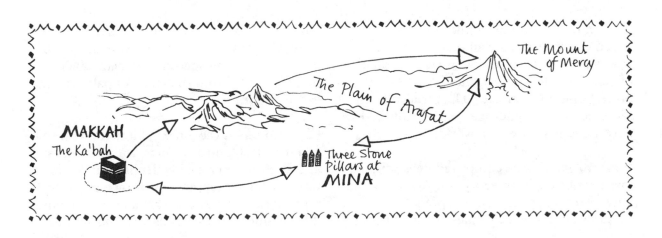

After Mina, pilgrims head back to Makkah. They will circle the Ka'bah another seven times at the close of pilgrimage, just as they had done when they started it.

Id-ul-Adha

As the rituals come to a close, pilgrims shave or shorten their hair in preparation for the Festival of Sacrifice 'Id-ul-Adha'. Once the feast begins pilgrims may change into normal clothes and start to celebrate the festival, which begins on the 10th of Dhul Hijjah – the first of four festival days.

During the festival each pilgrim must purchase and sacrifice an animal, usually a cow, sheep, goat or camel, in remembrance of Abraham and his sacrifice of the ram in place of his son Ishmael. The meat of all the sacrifices is then packaged and distributed to poor people all over the world.

With the pilgrimage completed, most pilgrims make a further journey to visit Madinah, the City of the Prophet (see Chapters 5 & 6). Madinah is about 227 miles to the north of

Makkah. Once there, pilgrims visit the Prophet's mosque and shrine, as well as shop for gifts to take home to family and friends.

The Festival of Sacrifice

Muslims throughout the world celebrate the pilgrimage festival 'Id-ul-Adha', remembering the story of Abraham and Ishmael, and celebrating the completion of the pilgrimage. Here are some descriptions from different countries.

Bahrain

Bahrain is an island close to Saudi Arabia.

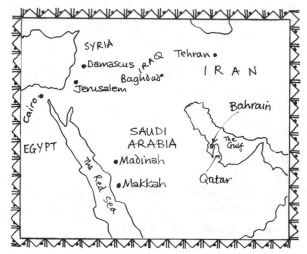

On the first of Dhul Hijjah, a basket-weaver or trader goes round the streets and between the houses selling specially shaped, small baskets woven from the reeds of palm trees, called 'gufahs'.

Children buy these gufahs, fill them with soil and compost, and sow them with the seeds of fast growing crops like lentils, parsley or wheat. All children have their own gufah to take care of, water, and check on its growth throughout the first ten days of this month.

The gufahs are hung on the wall in a string net.

On the tenth day of Dhul Hijjah, all the families of Bahrain go out to the seashore with their gufahs. The children recite a special rhyme asking the small plant in the gufah to go in their place on pilgrimage to Makkah, and after finishing the song; the gufahs are hurled into the water and float away towards Makkah. The gufah tradition is also practised in other Gulf States.

My Pilgrimage Plant

This is a translation of the song the children sing:

Go in my place on the pilgrimage
A pilgrimage has passed and another will be

On it have a safe journey
And then please ask this for me

May my acts be good and accepted by God
And may my conscience be clear

I have fed you supper, I have fed you lunch
So on the Id, say my prayer

Have a safe journey my pilgrimage plant!
Have a safe journey my pilgrimage plant!

175

Children compete throughout the first 10 days of Dhul Hijjah to see whose plant grows most, and who manages to throw his plant furthest out into the sea. It is best to throw the gufah a long way, as it will have a better chance of being carried out to sea towards Makkah.

Bangladesh

On the first day of Id-ul-Adha animals are sacrificed after the morning prayers. Some of the meat is cooked for the family lunch, and some is divided up into packets and given to the poor.

One friend recalled:

'Last time I visited my village, me and my brothers bought 4 cows, and divided up the meat into 200 packets which were distributed in the village. There are no fridges there so meat must be cooked and eaten quickly. It was a great chance to show generosity.'

Ishmael and Abraham

Below is a Bangladeshi folk version of the tale of Ishmael and Abraham. It is not a version recorded in the holy books, but is commonly told in some communities there:

One day God spoke to Abraham: 'You must give up the thing that you treasure most,' he said.

Abraham thought long and hard about what this might mean, finally realising that his son Ishmael was the thing he valued most.

Abraham took Ishmael out into the desert in order to kill him in a quiet place, and did not tell his son where they were going or why. On the way the devil whispered into Ishmael's ears:

'Your father is going to kill you! Your father is going to kill you!' But Ishmael threw stones at the devil and ignored him.

Three times the devil whispered this, and three times Ishmael threw stones at him. This is remembered, during the Hajj ceremony, by throwing stones at three pillars where it was said to have happened.

When they were at the chosen place, Abraham told his son that he planned to kill him, as God had commanded it.

Ishmael said, 'Father, if that is God's will, then you must do it!'

Abraham wanted to blindfold and tie him down, but Ishmael said,

'No, this sacrifice is not against my will. I will have neither blindfold nor ropes to bind me.'

Abraham pressed the knife against his son's neck but could not bring himself to cut into his son's flesh.

Ishmael cried out: 'Do it, father! Do as you have been commanded!'

Abraham could not bring himself to do it. In frustration he struck a large rock with the knife, and it cut straight though the rock with one stroke.

'Father, you wear the blindfold!' cried Ishmael, 'then you won't see my suffering!'

Abraham agreed, tied a blindfold over his eyes, and took a firm hold of his son.

He was about to slit his son's throat when God's voice spoke again:

'You have succeeded Abraham! I am pleased with you: take off your blindfold!'

Abraham pulled off the blindfold and saw that he was holding – not his son – but a ram. Ishmael was standing to one side and smiling. Abraham sacrificed the ram and praised God for his mercy.

Iraq

When a pilgrim arrives home from Makkah he/she is received at the outskirts of the neighbourhood by well-wishers with drums and coloured flags. The pilgrim is escorted home with songs and chants in praise of God.

When pilgrims return home, the family welcomes them with joy, kissing their hand in acknowledgement of their new status for having performed such an important religious duty.

For three days after the return of the pilgrim the family opens their house to visitors and congratulators. Large meals are offered and much cooking is done. On the third day of celebrations a special 'Mawood ceremony' is performed (a celebration of the Prophet's birth, life, and works, see Chapter 2), a form of celebration carried out at special times of the year in addition to the Prophet's birthday. The 'Mawood' celebrations involve the chanting and singing of religious songs in praise of God and his prophet.

Pilgrims usually bring presents for their family, relatives, and friends from Makkah. These include prayer rugs, rosary beads, incense, samples of water from the well of 'Zamzam', kohl for the eyes (eyeliner), male head-caps, and women's headscarves.
On the first day of the festival, after going to the mosque and visiting relatives, families who can afford it normally slaughter a sheep. They divide the meat into three portions, one for their own household; one for their relatives; and one third for the poor in their community. The family's portion is cooked and served on that first day.

Palestine

A Palestinian woman recalled her memories of the festival in her village in northern Palestine:

'For us the story of Abraham represents the idea of giving things up. That's why the festival is all about giving. We used to cut the sheep into three pieces, one third for the poor, one third to the relatives and one third stayed in the house.

The children had the job of deciding which portion went to which group: the meat was divided into three piles, and the children played a game with their eyes closed to decide which pile was for which group. Then my mother and brothers would divide up the meat for relatives and the poor into pieces, each in its own bag, and we would distribute it to relatives and the poor.

The children participated in distributing the food, and I had a really good feeling of helping and giving as we distributed the meat. In those days meat was something special as we were poor, and many families could never eat meat except at the festival. Also the gift of the meat showed that the giver was thinking about the person who received the gift. This gave a wonderful warm feeling of connection and community.'

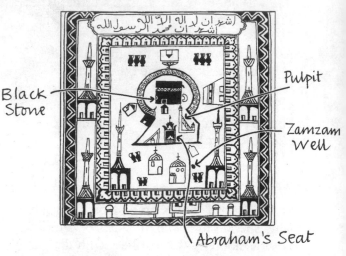

Black Stone

Pulpit

Zamzam Well

Abraham's Seat

Activity Ideas

✦ Learning the pilgrimage plant song
✦ Designing and colouring a ceramic tile with a map of the Ka'bah
✦ Planting a pilgrimage plant and sending it toward Makkah
✦ Making a card for Id-ul-Adha
✦ Cooking Qatayef Bel-Assel (honey pancakes)

Activity 1: learning the pilgrimage plant song

See p. 175 for tune: teach the song as a chant with clapping to help with the rhythm. It can also be taught using call and response (i.e. the caller chants the first line and then the group repeats the line). If you like, make up your own tune or chant.

Activity 2: designing and colouring a ceramic tile with a map of the Ka'bah

The design of this tile was made in 16th century Turkey. It shows the Ka'bah, the six minarets of the holy mosque, Abraham's Sanctuary, the Well of Zamzam (created by God to save Ishmael from dying of thirst), a pulpit for preaching, and other features related to the pilgrimage site.

Materials:

White or cream ceramic tiles, at least 2, (one for practising and testing colours), size 15cm x 15cm. If you have any other size, alter the pattern to fit it. (Tiles of all sizes can be purchased from B&Q, Homebase, and similar DIY stores.)

'Cold' ceramic colours (can be purchased from art shops). Make sure that you purchase the type that becomes permanent when dry and does not need to be fired in a kiln or heated in any way. **Please note:** these colours are only permanent if you do not expose the item you paint to hot soaking, for instance by putting the item in a dishwasher or in hot water for some time. You can wash them using ordinary detergents.

White spirit for cleaning the paintbrushes and any spillage etc. (This is a solvent, poisonous if swallowed, but perfectly safe if used under adult supervision).

Brushes

Carbon paper

Ballpoint pen

Sellotape

Cutter (stencil knife)

Plate stand, appropriate size for displaying the tile

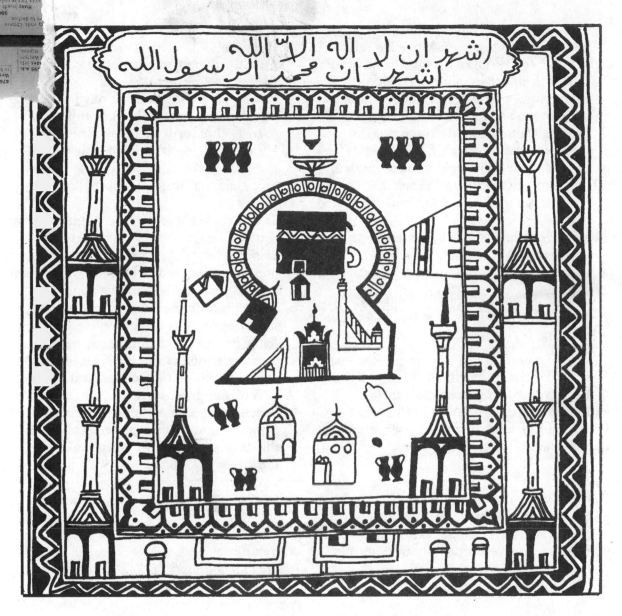

Method:

1 Wash and dry the tile, making sure that the surface to be painted is grease- and finger-print free.

2 Photocopy the tile design from the book and cut it to size.

3 Place the tile on a piece of card (so that you can move the tile around as you draw and colour without needing to touch it).

4 Place the carbon paper on the tile and fix with tape.

5 Place the design sheet on top of the carbon paper and fix with tape.

6 Trace out the design using the ballpoint pen, pressing down firmly to ensure that the design has been transferred.

7 Remove the paper and carbon sheet to reveal the traced design.

8 Decide on your colours and start colouring in the tile, making sure not to smudge the surface. It would be advisable to colour in stages, allowing the colour to dry or firm a little before adding other colours next to it.

9 Make sure that you clean the brushes regularly and thoroughly. If the paint dries on them, they will need to be discarded.

10 On completing your colouring, leave the tile to dry for 24 hours in a well-ventilated room.

11 You can display the tile by standing it on a plate stand or framing it.

Activity 3: planting a pilgrimage plant and sending it toward Makkah

This activity needs the support and supervision of an adult, especially for the last stage. It would be best to begin 10–15 days before Id-ul-Adha (the Pilgrimage Id), to experience caring for a small plant and the joy of sending it off down the river or across the sea towards Makkah.

Materials:

Seeds of either lentils, chick peas, wheat, parsley, or any other suitable fast-growing plants
Compost and a very small plastic plant pot to fit the basket
Small bamboo or wicker basket
String

Method:

1 Using the string, make long handles for the basket, so that it can be hung off a wall or a ledge.

2 Place the plant pot in the basket.

3 Add compost and plant the seeds.

4 Follow the instructions for the seeds. Make sure that you water the plant as advised in the instructions. Take care of the plant and monitor its progress.

5 With adult supervision, on the eve of the Pilgrimage Id or 'Id-ul-Adha', take the basket with its contents to the edge of a river or the seashore nearest to you. When you are there, think of all the things God has given you. Thank Him for your good health, for your family, and thank Him for helping you take loving care of the small plant.

6 Sing the pilgrimage plant song, or read it out.

7 Throw the basket with its contents as far as you can into the water, so that it can be carried away by the current or on the waves, hopefully towards Makkah, where Abraham built the house for God's worship.

8 If you fail to throw the plant far enough, you must not try to retrieve it, no matter how tempted you may be. God has received your dedication of the plant, and He knows your intentions and feelings, and will reward you generously for your efforts.

9 When you get back home, you may want to write about your experience of doing this activity and your reflections on the trip to the river or sea.

Activity 4: making a card for Id-ul-Adha

Materials:

White and coloured card (200g A4 size)
Colouring pens, pencils, or pastels
Scissors
Ruler
Pencil
Carbon paper
Stencil knife or cutter

Method:

1 Fold the A4 card in half.

2 Draw the design of the door on the intended cover. You may want to trace the design using carbon paper.

3 Open the card flat on the table.

Make a Pilgrimage Id Greetings Card

1) Fold A4 size card in half
2) Draw a design of a door on the Cover.
   You may wish to trace the design below

Design can be photocopied and stuck onto front of card
The Arabic Script reads: "HAPPY ID"

عيد سعيد

3) Open card flat and 4) Colour design.
5) Cut open the door along dotted lines

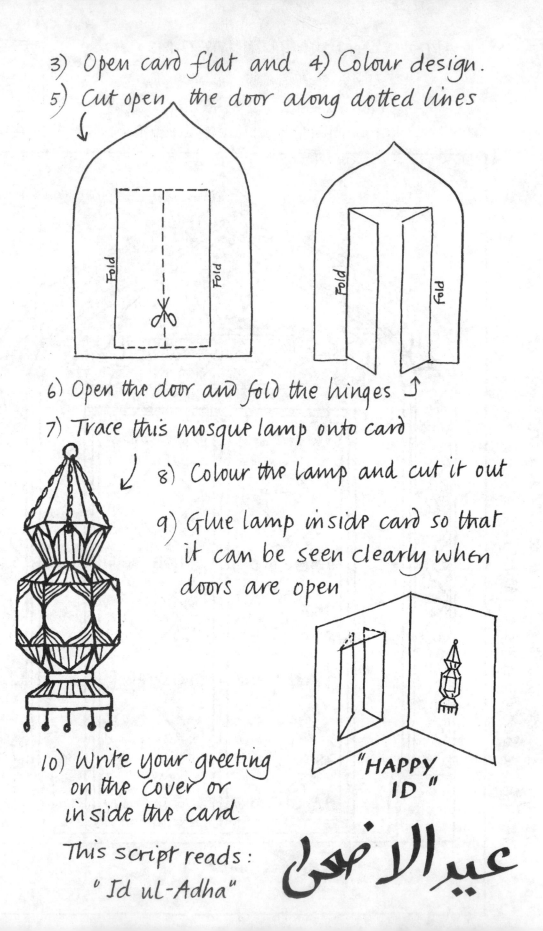

6) Open the door and fold the hinges ↱

7) Trace this mosque lamp onto card

8) Colour the lamp and cut it out

9) Glue lamp inside card so that
   it can be seen clearly when
   doors are open

"HAPPY
ID "

10) Write your greeting
    on the Cover or
    inside the card

This script reads:
    " Id ul-Adha"

عيد الاضحى

4 Colour the design.
5 Cut open the door in the design, following the dotted lines.
6 Open the door and fold the hinges.
7 Trace the mosque-lamp onto the card.
8 Colour the lamp and cut it out.
9 Glue the lamp inside the card, making sure that it is in a correct position for the door on the cover to be opened to reveal the lamp.
10 Write your greeting on the cover or inside.

Activity 5: cooking Qatayef Bel-Assel (honey pancakes)

Ingredients:
1 cup white flour
1 egg
3/4 cup milk
2 tablespoons honey
2 tablespoons vegetable oil
1/2 teaspoon baking powder
1/4 teaspoon salt
1 cup double cream
Grated walnuts

Method:
1 In a bowl mix together the flour, baking powder, and salt.
2 In a separate bowl, mix together the honey, egg, milk, and oil.
3 Making a hole in the centre of the flour mixture, gradually add the honey and milk liquid and mix with a spoon. Then beat the mixture until all is well blended. The mixture is ready for pancake making.
4 Heat a non-stick pan on the stove, greasing it with a little oil.
5 Using a large serving spoon, measure out a spoon of the pancake liquid and spread it out on the pan, making a circular pancake. Once the upper side forms a bubbly surface, turn the pancake over to be cooked on the other side as well.
6 Position the cooked pancake in a dish, roll and sprinkle with the grated walnuts, and serve hot with cream.

Optional: you may wish to add some sugar syrup or extra honey.

Stories about Equality and Justice

One of the important messages of Islam is equality: all have the right to justice and fairness. Whatever the status or wealth of an individual, all will one day die and be held to account for their lives. This is emphasised in the Hajj, when all pilgrims wear the same simple robes so that symbols of wealth and status are forgotten during the pilgrimage. Here are some folktales from around the Muslim world on the theme of equality.

Juha's Sleeve

Once Juha arrived at a royal banquet dressed in scruffy old rags. When the guards saw how poorly Juha was dressed they refused to let him enter the grand banquet hall. Juha went home, changed into his best clothes, and was allowed into the banquet hall immediately. He sat down close to the king and started eating. First he took a handful of rice and put it in his mouth, then he took a second handful and smeared it over his jacket.

'Enjoy it, you deserve it!' he muttered under his breath.

Next he ate a bite of chicken, but then smeared chicken fat all over his jacket. Again he muttered:

'Enjoy it, you deserve it!'

Then came a mouthful of soup, after which he poured the soup over himself, with the same words:

'Enjoy it, you deserve it!'

By this time everyone in the hall had stopped eating. They were all watching Juha cover his jacket in food. After a while the king shouted at Juha:

'Stop it, man. Stop wasting good food on your clothes. Food is for eating, not for smearing on your clothes!'

'No, your majesty,' replied Juha. 'My jacket deserves the food more than me. Without my jacket I would not be eating here, so it is only right that my jacket has its fair share!'

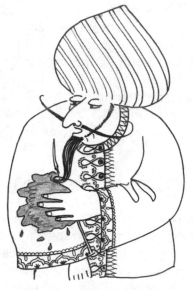

The Price of a Slap

This is another story written by Rumi, the great poet and storyteller born in 1207 AD in Balkh (modern day Afghanistan).

Once there was a thin, weak old man. He noticed that every day he grew weaker and thinner, and so one day he went to see a doctor to find out what was wrong.

'What did you eat today?' asked the Doctor.

'Why nothing' replied the old man.

'And yesterday?' asked the doctor.

'Nothing' replied the old man again, 'I have no money to buy food!'

The doctor felt sorry for the old man who was too poor to eat regularly. He thought for a minute and then said:

'The cure for your illness is to eat whatever you feel like and do whatever you feel like. Do that, and you will be cured.'

'Well thank you!' said the old man and left the doctor's house.

The old man was happy. All his life he had tried to do his duty. Now he could do whatever he liked!

The old man went for a walk down by the river, and after a while he passed a fisherman sitting on the banks of the river, holding a fishing rod. For some unknown reason the old man got an urge to slap the fisherman on the back of the neck. Remembering the words of the doctor, he did it! He gave the fisherman a hefty whack on the back of the neck, knocking the poor man into the river.

The fisherman was extremely angry when he pulled himself out of the river and back onto the shore, dripping wet and with a very sore neck.

'Why in God's name did you slap me?' he shouted at the old man.

'I don't know,' he replied in a puzzled way. 'I just felt like it.'

'You just felt like it! You just felt like it! We'll see about that. You can't just go around hitting people when you feel like it. You're coming to the judge with me. He'll sort you out!'

And so the fisherman marched the thin, old man to the court to see the judge.

'Your honour, this man slapped me on the back of the neck and knocked me into the river. I demand justice!'

'I see,' replied the judge, 'this little old man knocked you into the river. Tell me old man, why did you do it?'

'I don't know,' he replied in the same puzzled way. 'I really don't know, I just felt like it.'

'He must pay a fine!' shouted the fisherman.

'I'll be the judge of that,' said the judge. 'Tell me old man, how much money do you have?'

'Nothing', he replied.

'And how many animals do you own?'

'None'.

'And how much land?'

'None'.

Then the judge began to feel sorry for the old man.

'My dear fisherman. See how poor this old man is. He is weak and thin from hunger. Do you really seek to punish him more?'

'Well he can't go around just slapping people when he wants to!' snapped the fisherman.

'No, but maybe he would stop if he wasn't so hungry,' said the judge. 'What about you, fisherman? How much money do you have on you now?'

'Why do you want to know?' asked the fisherman suspiciously.

'I am the judge. It's my job to ask, and yours to answer, so tell me. How much?'

The fisherman checked his pockets.

'I have twenty dinars, your honour.'

'Good. Then my decision is that you should give ten dinars to this poor man who has no money, and keep the other ten for yourself. That would be fair as the man is so poor.'

'Fair! Fair! What is fair about that? He slaps me and I have to pay him ten dinars. That is not fair, that is foolish!'

The judge went bright red in the face and glared at the fisherman.

'How dare you say that to me? I am the judge. You should show more respect or you will find yourself in jail!'

The fisherman and the judge began to argue, while the old man listened.

The old man thought to himself:

'Hmmm, so one slap is worth ten dinars!'

Just then his eyes were caught by the back of the judge's neck, and he got a strange urge to slap the neck. Remembering his doctor's advice, he did it. He slapped the back of the judge's neck knocking him onto the floor.

The fisherman gave a big grin and slapped down twenty dinars on the judge's table.

'Take them,' he said to the old man 'That's ten for the first and ten for the second slap.'

'What?' roared the judge from the floor. 'Are you paying him to slap me?'

'Absolutely,' replied the grinning fisherman. 'If it's right for me then it must be right for you too. I wish I had more money, then I'd pay for another ten of those slaps. Maybe then you'd learn that what's right for others should also be right for yourself.'

How the Cockerel Got his Coin Back

This folktale from Iraq is great for young children, who can join in with the cockadoodledoo when it's time to wake the king!

Once there was a little cockerel. The little cockerel lived in a little cottage with a very tiny and very kind old lady. They were very happy but very poor. Every day the cockerel would go down to the bottom of the cottage garden and go scritching and scratching around in the soil, looking for something to eat.

One day he was scritching and scratching around when he saw something glittering on the ground. It was a gold coin!

The little cockerel was so happy. 'I'll give the coin to my kind old lady, and then we can buy a real feast,' he thought.

Just then the king came walking down the street past the house, dressed in fine clothes of silk and velvet. He saw the gold coin, stepped over the fence, picked it up and put it in his pocket.

'That's not fair!' shouted the cockerel. That's my coin. Give it back! That's not fair!'

But the king paid no attention. He stepped back over the fence and walked away back to the palace.

That evening the king was going to bed. He got into his silk pyjamas, put on his velvet sleeping hat, slipped under his soft clean sheets and put his head down on a pillow of the finest softest feathers. He was just dropping off to sleep when the little cockerel hopped up onto his bedroom windowsill.

'Cockadoodledoo! Cockadoodledoo!

I'll shout and sing
With all my might
You took my coin
And that's not right
Cockadoodledoo! Cockadoodledoo!'

'Guards, guards,' shouted the king, 'get rid of this cockerel. I'm trying to sleep.'

Two guards came in, grabbed the cockerel by the neck, and took it outside into the palace gardens. In the garden was a big water tank with a heavy lid on top.

They opened the lid, threw the cockerel inside and shut the door again, thinking that the cockerel would drown.

But the clever, brave little cockerel opened his mouth and GLUG GLUG GLUG GLUG he swallowed all the water in the tank!

When the guards came back a while later and lifted the lid of the tank, the little cockerel flapped his wings and flew up past them, up into the sky.

A while later the king was snoring loudly, his four fat chins wobbling backwards and forwards as he slept. He was just in the middle of a delightful dream about a wonderful feast of food, when …

'Cockadoodledoo! Cockadoodledoo!
I'll shout and sing
With all my might
You took my coin
And that's not right
Cockadoodledoo! Cockadoodledoo!'

'Guards, guards,' shouted the king. Get rid of this cockerel. I'm trying to sleep.'

Three guards came in, grabbed the cockerel by the neck, and took him down to the place kitchens.

In the kitchen was a huge oven, full of burning wood. They opened the oven door, threw the cockerel inside and closed the door, thinking they would be eating roast cockerel for supper.

But the clever little cockerel, the brave little cockerel ...he opened his mouth and SSSSSSSSSS... out came all the water he had drunk in the tank, putting out the fire and cooling down the oven till the cockerel was quite cool.

A while later when the guards came back and opened the oven door, expecting to find their supper, the little cockerel flapped his wings and flew up past them, out of the kitchen window and up into the sky.

A while later the king was in the middle of a dream about gold and jewels. He was counting all of his money, coin by coin when...

'Cockadoodledoo! Cockadoodledoo!
I'll shout and sing
With all my might
You took my coin

And that's not right
Cockadoodledoo! Cockadoodledoo!'

'Guards, guards,' called the king, 'get rid of this cockerel. I'm trying to sleep.'

Four guards came in, grabbed the cockerel by the neck, and took him down to the bottom of the palace gardens. They walked up to a large white wooden box with the sound of buzzing coming from it... a beehive. The guards opened the top of the beehive and threw the cockerel inside, and then closed the top again, thinking the cockerel would get stung to death. But the clever little cockerel, the brave little cockerel ...he opened his mouth and GAH, GAH, GAH, GAH, GAH. He swallowed all the bees in the beehive.

Later, when the guards came back and opened the beehive door, expecting to find their supper, the little cockerel flapped his wings and flew up past them, out of the kitchen window and up into the sky.

A while later the King was just in the middle of a dream about cockerels, when...

'Cockadoodledoo! Cockadoodledoo!
I'll shout and sing
With all my might
You took my coin
And that's not right
Cockadoodledoo! Cockadoodledoo!'

'Guards, guards,' called the King, 'get rid of this cockerel. I'm trying to sleep.'

Five guards came in and tried to grab the cockerel, but this time he was too quick for them, flapped his wings and circled above them close to the ceiling. The guards started jumping up trying to catch the cockerel, knocking over the chairs, tables, mirrors and vases as they jumped.

Then the clever little cockerel, the brave little cockerel ...he opened his mouth and CA...CA....CA...CA.....CA ....all of those bees he had swallowed came buzzing out of his mouth and started stinging the guards who were trying to catch him.

'OWWW! OWWW! Your majesty, I've got stung on the elbow!' cried one.

'OOOOOCH! My leg hurts!' cried another.

'OH NO! MY NOSE!' cried a third.

Imagine the racket: five guards jumping around the king's bedroom, wailing about their bee-stings.

The king had had enough!

'QUIET!' he shouted. 'Guards, go and get that gold coin and give it to the cockerel, or I'll never get any sleep!'

So the guards gave the coin back and the cockerel took it home to the kind little old lady. She was so happy. She went shopping and they had a fantastic feast of the most delicious food, and lived happily ever after.

Juha's Nail

Juha's nail is so well known throughout the Muslim world that the phrase 'Juha's Nail' has become a proverb in its own right. If someone puts a condition in a contract that will cause trouble later a businessman might say, 'I can't agree to that. That's like Juha's Nail!'

Juha lived in a fine big house, while his neighbour lived in a smaller one. One day the neighbour decided to try and persuade Juha to sell his house by making his life miserable. First the neighbour got up every night and made as much noise as possible, banging pots and pans and singing at the top of his voice.

Juha got out of bed and called out of his window asking his neighbour to be quiet.

'Sorry, I can't,' his neighbour shouted back, 'I have to make noise at night. I can't help it. But if you would like to sell me your house, that would be fine with me. After all, the neighbourhood is getting noisy!'

Juha said he would think about it.

A week went by, and every night the noise continued. Then one morning a pile of rubbish appeared in Juha's garden. He knew it was from his neighbour, but when he mentioned it, the neighbour just said that the neighbourhood was going downhill, and why didn't Juha consider moving?

All week the noise continued in the night, and every morning there was fresh rubbish in Juha's garden.

Then one afternoon, when Juha was walking past his neighbour's house, the neighbour threw a bucket of dirty water out of the doorway, right onto Juha's head.

'Oops,' said the neighbour, 'Didn't see you there'.

Juha said nothing and went home to change.

The neighbour couldn't believe his luck. He had got the house, and for half price, so he readily agreed. Lawyers were brought in, signing over the house, but giving Juha rights to his nail.

The next evening, the neighbour was fast asleep in his new home, when there was a knock at the door. Half asleep, the neighbour opened the door to find Juha on his doorstep.

'I've come to visit my nail,' smiled Juha.

'Can't you come back in the morning?' asked the neighbour.

'Nope, I need to see it now.'

'This is a nuisance,' thought the neighbour, 'but for 10,000 dinars saved, it was worth it.' The neighbour went back to bed, and Juha went to see his nail.

In the morning the neighbour woke to a disgusting smell. He and his wife went downstairs and found, hanging on the nail, a pair of rotten old boots, smelling like a rubbish dump and teeming with maggots and slugs. The smell was terrible throughout the house – but well, for 10,000 dinars they would put up with it.

The next day he went to visit his neighbour and told him he was ready to sell.

'How much will you give me for my house?' asked Juha.

'Twenty thousand dinars,' replied the neighbour, very pleased that his plan had worked.

'Fine,' replied Juha, 'I'll sell it to you for half, for ten thousand dinars.'

'Why?' asked the astonished neighbour.

'Well, the thing is, there is the matter of my nail. You see, in the house there is a nail. It belonged to my father and before that to his father and I am very fond of it. I am willing to sell you my house, but on the condition that I keep the nail. It's stuck in the wall in the front room. I want to be able to visit the nail whenever I want, and hang whatever I want on it, to honour the memory of my father and grandfather. Agree to that, whenever I wish, and I'll give you the house for half price.'

A few nights later there was another midnight knock on the door – Juha again.

'O thank God you're back,' said the neighbour. 'Please take away the boots!'

'Yes I'm planning to take them away,' said Juha, shuffling towards his nail.

'Good,' said the neighbour and went back to bed.

The next morning the neighbour woke up itching all over. His body was covered in little insect bites which itched like mad. His wife and children were also covered in bites.

They looked around for the source and found an old jacket hanging up on Juha's nail. The jacket was actually light green, but it was covered in so many fleas that from a distance it seemed black. The fleas were hungry and jumped at any warm-blooded creature they could find. Juha's neighbour washed and scrubbed the house all day, but more and more fleas kept jumping off the coat, keeping his whole family awake every night for a week.

At the end of the week there was a knock on the door in the middle of the night. 'Please, please!' begged the neighbour, 'please take away that jacket. It's driving me mad!'

'Oh I am sorry to hear that,' replied Juha with a smile, 'you'll be pleased to hear I'm going to take it away.'

Juha went to his nail and replaced the coat with two rotten, old fish. If the boots had smelt bad, the fish were a hundred times worse. Everything in the house smelt of rotten fish, the children smelt so bad they were sent home from school, and the man smelt so bad nobody would buy from his shop.

The man had had enough – he went off to find Juha.

'Please,' he begged, 'buy your house back. It's unbearable for us to live there with that nail of yours. Please take it back!'

And so Juha bought his house back for half the price he had been paid for it, and his neighbour never tried to get rid of him again.

Afterword

Many illustrations appear throughout this book. Some are decorative, some use images of people and animals to tell a story, and some accompany and explain the craft activities. All these illustrations were designed and chosen after much consideration and reflection on the issue of Islam and the depiction of human and animal images in all art forms. The issue of whether to use such images or not will no doubt always be controversial, especially for images that represent prophets and angels.

As a Muslim I would like to personally assure all my brothers and sisters in the faith that all images in this book were created solely to meet the educational needs that inspired this publication. They are not a mere end in themselves, nor meant to be used in any form or act of worship, nor to accurately depict human or angel beings. Instead, the illustrations are meant to help educate children, especially non-Muslim children seeking a better understanding of Islam, in an accessible, imaginative and enjoyable way.

Times are currently very difficult for the Muslim world, so we should seize every opportunity to offer true insight into a religion that has been greatly misinterpreted, manipulated and distorted by many different groups who are motivated by a variety of political and ideological interests.

To keep within the spirit of Islam and its views on image creation, we have consciously designed illustrations to be cartoon-like figures for illustrating the main text and stories. We have chosen to depict the angels and the Prophet Muhammad, peace be upon him, based on such representations in traditional Islamic miniatures and manuscripts. We genuinely hope that these will not be offensive: the aim behind them is a noble one, that of sharing knowledge and enjoyment of Islamic festivals, culture and beliefs.

I have found that exploring the diversity of Islamic festivals, customs, and traditions throughout the Islamic world has reaffirmed for me the true spirit of my faith as a flexible religion, full of joy and happiness, as well as an inspiration for piety and righteousness – relevant today as it has been through the ages.

I hope readers will enjoy this book as much as we have enjoyed researching it.

Noorah Al-Gailani

About the Illustrator

Helen Williams has been interested in Islam and fascinated by Islamic design for nearly thirty years. During this period she has worked as an artist, illustrator and teacher. Helen has travelled widely but feels most 'at home' in the Middle East.

Helen has used references from a wide variety of sources for this book. Ideas and design have come from Islamic illustrations and paintings, ceramics, textiles, metalwork and architecture. She has consulted Muslim friends and observed Islamic communities in England, India, Turkey and Egypt. Helen has endeavoured to use appropriate material that honours and respects the diversities of multicultural Islam.

Appendix 1

The Festival of Ashura and the Sunni/Shi'ah Schism

When the Prophet Muhammad died in 632 AD, his followers were distraught and confused. Abu Bakr, the Prophet's best friend and the father of Aisha, the Prophet's wife, called out to all the assembled in the Madinah mosque and said:

'O people, those of you who worshipped Muhammad, Muhammad has died. And those of you who worshipped God, God is ever living.' He then recited this verse from the Qur'an:

'Muhammad is no more than a Messenger; many were the messengers that passed away before him. If he died or were slain, will you turn back on your heels? If any did turn back on his heels, not the least harm will he do to God; but God will reward those thankful believers.'

The Qur'an: *Surat Al-Imran.*

The Prophet had died without nominating a successor in leading the fledgling community. A leader was needed, and Abu Bakr was elected for this role. The position came to be known as Caliph (the Prophet's representative). The Caliph was to lead the Muslim community (Ummah) in all matters of life – except for prophethood, which had been completed with the death of Muhammad. Abu Bakr and the following three Caliphs were chosen democratically by a group of Muslim leaders who were present in Madinah at that time.

The first four Caliphs were religious men who had previously been close companions of the Prophet. The fourth one, Ali, was Muhammad's first cousin and son-in-law. During the period of his rule the city of Kufah in southern Iraq became the capital of the expanding empire. In 661 AD, Ali was assassinated on his way to the mosque in Kufah.

With Ali's death a new era in the Caliphate began. Muawiya, the governor of Syria, was chosen to be the next Caliph. Muawiya broke tradition by deciding to nominate his own son Yazid to be his successor, the next Caliph. By doing so he established the first Islamic monarchy, the Umayyads.

The Ummayads supervised Islam's expansion into new territories: Central Asia, North Africa, and Spain. They chose Damascus in Syria as their capital. However, during the early years of Ummayad rule, there was a vigorous debate within the Muslim community relating to their legitimacy. Some argued that only members of Muhammad's direct descendants were fit to be Caliphs, and so recognised Ali as the last of the true Caliphs and demanded that his sons Al-Hasan and Al-Husayn be Caliphs. This group became known as Shi'at Ali (Ali's followers), or the Shi'ah.

When Muawiya died in 680 AD, his court and supporters sought acknowledgement and pledges of allegiance for his son Yazid. Most did oblige, but the Shi'ah and Al-Husayn refused to recognise Yazid as the next Caliph. The Shi'ah in Iraq invited Al-Husayn, Ali's son, to come to Iraq from Madinah, to lead them against Yazid, and claim the Caliphat for himself.

Al-Husayn left Madinah for Kufa in Iraq with his household, family and some followers. There were 200 in all. Yazid heard of Husayn's intentions and sent an army of four thousand to meet them. On the 10th of Muharram (10th October 680 AD), Husayn reached Karbala in Iraq, some 25 miles from Kufa, where Yazid's army met them.

The people of Kufah who had persuaded Husayn to come, failed to turn up for the decisive battle. Husayn and his family were left to fight for their principles on their own. The battle took most of the day, with many heroic acts from Husayn's camp, but in the end all the men were killed, sparing only women and children, including Husayn's son Ali Zain-Al-Abedin. Husayn's head was cut off and later buried with his body. The site of Al-Husayn's burial is one of the most important Shi'ah shrines today.

The battle of 10th Muharram is known as Ashura. The word is derived from the name of the number 10 in Arabic: Asharah. The martyrdom of Al-Husayn and his family is commemorated annually all over the Islamic world, and especially where there are Shi'ah communities. The pageants of Ashura, enacting the events and battle scenes leading up to the death of Al-Husayn, are similar to those celebrating Christ's passion at Easter.

This early schism between the majority of the Muslim population, the Sunni ('those who follow the Prophet's practices and tradition') and the Shi'ah ('the followers of Ali'), was mainly over the ideology of governorship of the Muslim community. In the following thirteen centuries after the death of Al-Husayn, the theology and doctrines of both sects developed to meet continually changing times. Sharia law was developed, new schools of thought in interpreting the life and work of the Prophet came into being, and offshoots and break-away factions appeared. Politics of the time, as well as theological and doctrinal issues, played a significant part in shaping the positively rich and diverse, though sometimes controversial, scene of Islam today. But despite this, there still exists an unbreakable golden thread of unity between all Muslims in the world, whose intertwined strings are: the One God, His Message, and His Prophet.

The festival of Ashura in Iraq

The 1st of Muharam (the Islamic New Year day) to 10th of Muharam (Ashur) are days especially commemorated amongst the Shi'ah, and some of the Sunnis in Iraq. This is a sombre festival recollecting the sad days of the betrayal and martyrdom of the Prophet's grandson, the Imam Al-Husayn and his family.

The commemorations take the form of a great pageant, with parades and processions in the main Shi'ah holy places and shrines in Baghdad, Kufa, Karbala and Najaf. The enactments carried out in the parades show the different stages and events leading to the final battle of 10th Muharam between the Umayyad army and Al-Husayn's group, and its aftermath. These pageants are carried out in full costume with each of the city's neighbourhoods or districts participating in a specific parade, including camels and horses, in which adults and children enact an episode of the story of Al-Husayn and his family's last ten days.

Those whose houses lie on the procession routes install 'Hibbs' (huge unglazed pottery drinking water vessels) on the pavements for passers-by to use.

'Herisah' (a wheat and meat-stock sweet dish) is made on this occasion. It is usually distributed amongst the participants in the pageant and the poor of the neighbourhood, or used as a votive offering on the fulfilment of a vow to God.

Throughout these ten days the more affluent households hire female reciters to read out the episodes of Al-Husayn's story in their homes.

On the seventh day, 'Khubs Al-Abbas' (a special bread) is made and eaten by the guests attending the recitations. It is offered with cheese, green herbs and salad vegetables.

And finally, on the last day of the anniversary, the 10th of Muharram, food is cooked on the streets, in gigantic pots on open fires, to be eaten there and then by all those participating in the festivities. The main dish prepared here consists of a mincemeat gravy and rice, 'Temen Qimah'.

The festivities of 'Mared Al-Rass'

This second part of the Ashura festival takes place 40 days after the 10th of Muharram. The main venue is the city of Karbala and the shrine of Al-Husayn there.

The festivities recall Al-Husayn's sister bringing back the severed head of Al-Husayn from Damascus to be interred with his body. On that day the Shi'ah Muslims of Iraq cook and distribute amongst their neighbours 'Zerdah wa Halib' (a sweet rice and milk dish).

The festival of Ashura in Malaysia

Ashura is a minor festival in Malaysia and Singapore. However, in the communities who celebrate this festival two main features are: fasting for the day, and cooking the Ashura porridge, known as 'Bubor Ashura'.

This Ashura porridge commemorates part of the Karbala battle events. Tradition has it that at the height of the battle at Karbala, the Makkan army of Husayn was reduced to its last rations. There was not enough food to go round, so it was decided to collect any food that was left, and to cook the whole lot for the soldiers. Many kinds of foodstuff were collected and cooked together as a porridge.

Malaysian Muslims re-enact this story in preparing the Ashura porridge. The person leading the cooking of the porridge receives food contributions from the neighbourhood and community to be used in the porridge. These contributions may include bananas, sugar, flour, maize, coconut, rice, dates – anything edible, even meat. All are used to make the porridge. Despite the strange mix of flavours, this ritual porridge is shared and eaten by all the community in remembrance of Karbala.

Appendix 2

Glossary

The Qur'an was revealed in Arabic, and so Arabic is the language of Islam, whatever the mother tongues spoken in a particular country. The transliterations used here are those recommended by the UK curriculum authority for teachers. They are not exact transliterations of the Arabic, but are intended to give a 'good enough' pronunciation for teaching purposes. Apostrophes are used to indicate a pause.

Al-Aqsa One of the mosques of Jerusalem

Ashura Shi'ah festival commemorating the martyrdom of Husayn

Al-hamdu-li-Llah 'All praise belongs to God', frequently used as a way of thanking God

Al-Madinah The name given to the city of Yathrib after the Prophet migrated there in 622 AD, and founded the first Islamic State

Adhan The call to prayer

Allah Arabic word for God

Angels Beings created by God from light

Arafat The plain, close to Makkah, where pilgrims gather to worship during the Hajj rituals

As-Salamu-Alaykum 'Peace be upon you', an Islamic greeting

Caliph The Prophet's representative, leader of the Islamic community

Hajar Wife of the prophet Abraham (Ibrahim), mother of Ishmael (Ismael)

Hajj Annual pilgrimage to Makkah, which each Muslim should undertake at least once in his or her lifetime if able. A male who has completed the pilgrimage is known as Hajji; a woman Hajjah

Hijrah Departure or emigration: used to describe the departure of the Prophet for Madinah, the date when the Islamic calendar begins

Ibrahim Abraham – father of Ishmael

Id Religious holiday

Id-ul-Adha Festival of the Sacrifice, commemorating Abraham's willingness to sacrifice his son for God. Also known as the Lesser Id

Id-ul-Fitr Festival of the breaking of the fast at the end of Ramadan

Islam Peace obtained through willing obedience to God's guidance

Isma'il Ishmael, son of Abraham

Jibril Gabriel, the angel who delivered God's message to Muhammad

Ka'bah Cube-shaped house at the centre of the Makkah grand mosque, the first house built for worship of the One God

Khadijah First wife of Muhammad

Laylat-ul-Qadr The Night of Destiny, when the first revelation was made to Muhammad

Makkah City where Muhammad was born

Mu'adhin The caller to prayer

Muhammad The Prophet. The name means 'praised'

Muslim Someone who has accepted Islam by professing the Shahadah

Qur'an The holy book revealed to the Prophet

Ramadan The ninth month on the Islamic calendar, when fasting is required from dawn to sunset

Salah Prayer: worship of God as prescribed by the Prophet

Sawm Fasting from before dawn until sunset

Shahadah Declaration of faith, by stating, 'There is no God except Allah, and Muhammad is the messenger of Allah'

Shi'ah Muslims who believe in the successorship of Ali (see Appendix 1)

Sunni The beliefs of mainstream Islam (as opposed to the Shi'ah), based on the Qur'an and the practices of the Prophet.

Surah Division of the Qur'an (also written as Surat)

Ummah The Muslim Community

Zakah Giving to the poor

Zamzam The holy well at Makkah

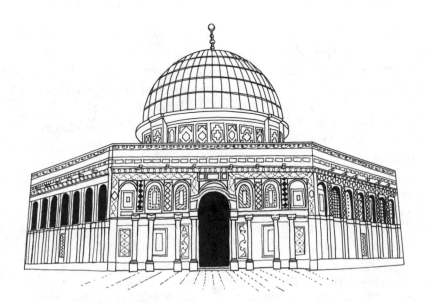

Appendix 3

References and Further Reading

Arabic titles

1 *Hayat Muhammed* (The Life of Mohammed), by Muhammed Husain Haikal, Egypt, 1935.

2 *Mukhtassar Seerat Ibin Hisham* (Ibin Hisham's condensed biography of the Prophet Muhammed), edited by Muhammed Afeef Al-Zuabi and Abd Al-Hamid Al-Ahdeb, published by Dar Al-Nafais, Beirut, Lebanon, 1993. Note: Ibin Hisham died in 793 A.D.

3 *Safwat Al-Tafasir, Tafsir lel-Qur'an Al-Karim*, ..., (The Finest of Commentaries, Interpretation of the Holy Qur'an, ...), by Muhammed Ali Al-Sabuni, published by Dar Al-Jeel, Beirut, Lebanon, and Dar Al-Sabuni, Cairo, Egypt, 1995.

4 *Qissas Al-Anbia* (The stories of the prophets in the Qur'an), by Abd Al-Wahab Al-Najar, published by Dar Al-Fikr, Beirut, Lebanon, 1934.

5 *Tarikh Al-Arab* (History of the Arabs), by Philip Hitti, published by Dar Ghandur, Beirut, Lebanon, 1986.

6 *Nidham Al-Islam, Al-Aqidah wa Al-Ibadah*, (The System of Islam, Belief and Worship), by Muhammed Al-Mubarak, published by Dar Al-Fikr, Beirut, Lebanon, 1984.

7 *Baghdad fi Al-Ishreenat* (Baghdad in the Twenties), by Abas Baghdadi, published by Dar Al-Shoon Al-Thaqafiah, Baghdad, Iraq, 2000.

8 *Murshid Al-Musali, le adaa faridhat al-salat wa-ma yetalaq beha min ahkam,* (The Worshipper's Guide to Prayer and its Stipulations), by Dawood Sabri Sulayman, published by the Religious Education Society, Baghdad, Iraq, 1980.

9 *Esalet Taalim Al-Salat,* (Treatise on how to Pray), by Najim Al-Din Al-Waidh, published by the Muslim Clerics Association, Baghdad, Iraq, 1980.

10 *Dalil Al-Tabikh wa Al-Taghthia* (The Guide to Cooking and nutrition), by Naziha Adib, Ferdous Al-Mukhtar, and Ban Ismail, published by Dar Al-Hikma, London, 1997.

Arabic-English titles

11 *The Holy Qur'an, and English translation of the meanings and commentary*, edited by The Presidency of Islamic Researches, Ifta, Call and Guidance, Al-Madinah Al-Munawarah, Saudi Arabia, 1990.

12 *Forty Hadith Qudsi,* translated by Ezzedin Ibrahim and Denys Johnson-Davies, Millat Book Centre, Abu Dhabi, UAE, 1979.

English titles

13 *The Architecture of The Holy Mosque, Makkah,* edited by Salma Samar Damluji, Hazar Publishing Ltd, London, 1998.

14 *Arab Painting*, by Richard Ettinghausen, Skira and Macmillan, London, 1977.

15 *The Koran*, translated with notes by N. J. Dawood, Penguin Books, London 1993.

16 *A History of The Arab Peoples*, by Albert Hourani, Faber and Faber, London, 1991.

17 *Islam, Art and Architecture*, edited by Markus Hattstein and Peter Delius, Konemann Verlagsgesellschaft mbH, Cologne, Germany, 2000.

18 *A modern guide to astronomical calculations of Islamic Calendar, Times and Qibla*, by Mohammad Ilyas, Berita Publishing Sdn. Bhd., Kuala Lumpur, Malaysia, 1984.

19 *Domestic Culture in The Middle East, an exploration of the household interior* by Jennifer Scarce, National Museums of Scotland, 1996.

20 *Ninety-Nine Names of Allah, The Beautiful Names,* by Shems Friedlander, Wildwood House Ltd., London 1978.

21 *Festivals of Malaya,* by Joy Manson, Donald Moore for Eastern Universities Press Ltd, Singapore, 1965.

Appendix 4

Sources of Craft Materials

The sources and products listed here are ones the authors used, but the list is not exhaustive. Manufacturers of products can advise on the closest retailer stocking their goods. Most of the craft materials shops have catalogues and/or take orders over the phone. Please note that this information was accurate at the time of publishing, but changes may have occurred since then.

Craft materials manufacturers and shops (most do mail-order)

Children's Book Centre
Has a large crafts materials section
237 Kensington High Street
London W8 6SA
Tel. (+44) (0)20 7937 7497
Fax. (+44) (0)20 7938 4968
Website: www.childrensbookcentre.co.uk

Book Ends
Books on crafts, etc.
17 Exhibition Road
London SW7 2HQ
Tel. (+44) (0)20 7589 2285

The Wheatsheaf Art Shop
56 Baker Street
London W1M 1DJ
Tel. (+44) (0)20 7935 5510
Fax. (+44) (0)20 7935 3794

Cowling & Wilcox Ltd.
Artists' supplies
26/28 Broadwick Street
London W1V 1FG
Tel. (+44) (0)20 7734 5781
Fax. (+44) (0)20 7434 4513

Alec Tiranti Ltd.
Sculptors' materials
27 Barren Street
London W1P 5DG
Tel. & fax. (+44) (0)20 7636 8565

Fashion 'n' Foil Magic
Mail order catalogue for textile colours
P.O. Box 3746
London N2 9DE
Tel. (+44) (0)20 8444 1992
Fax. (+44) (0)20 8883 0845

Edding (UK) Ltd.
Manufacturers of colours for craftwork, etc.
Merlin Centre,
Acrewood Way
St Albans
Herts. AL4 0JY
Tel. (+44) (0)1727 846688
Fax. (+44) (0)1727 839970

Pebeo (UK) Ltd.
Manufacturers of colours for craftwork, etc.
Unit 109 Solent Business Centre
Millbrook Road West
Millbrook
Southampton SO15 0HW
Tel. (+44) (0)2380 901914
Fax. (+44) (0)2380 901916
Website: www.pebeo.com

Pritt Childsplay range
Glitters, glues, glitzy bitz, and glaze
Henkel Home Improvement and Adhesive
Products
Winsford
Cheshire CW7 3QY
Tel. (+44) (0)1606 593933

Galt Products UK
Wide range of craft materials
Brookfield Road
Cheadle
Cheshire SK8 2PN
Tel. (+44) (0)161 428 9111
Fax. (+44) (0)161 428 6597

The Brighton Bead Shop
21 Sydney Street
Brighton BN1 4EN
Tel. (+44) (0)1273 675077
Fax. (+44) (0)1273 692803

Helios Fountain
Textile paints, glitter and other craft materials
7 Grassmarket
Edinburgh EH1 2HY
Tel. (+44) (0)131 229 7884
Fax. (+44) (0)131 622 7173
Website: www.helios-fountain.co.uk

Miller's Graphics
Card, paper, paints and other stationery
36 North Bridge
Edinburgh EH1 1QG
Tel. (+44) (0)131 225 1006
Fax. (+44) (0)131 225 8528

Miller's Graphics
Card, paper, paints and other stationery
265 Renfrew Street
Glasgow G3 6TT
Tel. (+44) (0)141 333 0188
Fax. (+44) (0)141 332 6012

Kernowcraft Rocks and Gems Ltd.
Good suppliers of beads, for the prayer bead activity
Bolingey
Perranporth
Cornwall TR6 ODH
Tel. (+44) (0)1872 573888
Fax. (+44) (0)1872 573704
Website: www.kernowcraft.com

P. J. Minerals
Good suppliers of beads, for the prayer bead activity
666A Liverpool Road
Ainsdale
Southport PR8 3LT
Tel. (+44) (0)1704 575461
Fax. (+44) (0)1704 576181
Website: www.beads.co.uk

Appendix 5

Further Resources

The IQRA Trust, London, offers a wide range of resource materials for use in UK schools.
Phone and they will send a catalogue.
IQRA Trust
24 Culross Street
London WIY 3HE
Tel. (+44) (0)20 7491 1572
Website: www.iqratrust.org,
for IQRA US publications see www.iqra.org

The Islamic Foundation offers a range of books, posters, pamphlets and multi-media resources for education about Islam.
Find your closest outlet, or order online through www.islamic-foundation.com or Tel. (+44) (0)1530 249230.
Has outlets worldwide.

The Muslim Educational Trust, London, also offers a useful range of resources for teachers.
Muslim Educational Trust
130 Stroud Green Road
London N4 3RZ
UK
Tel. (+44) (0)20 7272 8502

Appendix 6

Suggestions for Teachers

Each chapter in this book except chapter one contains four sections:

- An account of part of the life of the Prophet;
- a description of an associated festival and how it is celebrated in different Muslim countries;
- suggested activities for introducing the idea of the festival;
- folktales whose themes relate to the festival.

The idea of this scheme (see also schematic table in the Introduction) is to enable teachers to mix and match activities depending on the aims and needs of a particular group. The following are suggestions for possible ways of working:

✦ It will usually be a good idea to give the class, whatever their age, an outline of the life of the Prophet, so that any further teaching of religious belief or practice can be understood within the context of this wider story.

✦ One way to do this is to tell the whole of the Prophet's life in a first class, say in a fifty-minute telling, before going into details of specific practices or beliefs. Alternatively, the story could be told over a week, one section at a time.

✦ Once told, the story of the Prophet provides a variety of opportunities for discussion, re-enactment, writing, script writing, painting and poetry where this is appropriate. Such activities will deepen children's connection with these core stories.

✦ The teacher may then choose to introduce talk of specific religious practices associated either with Islam in general or with a specific festival/celebration. Muslims' faith is built directly on the words of the Qur'an and the life of the Prophet: the book layout enables children to clearly connect particular practices with one part of the prophet's life. The book emphasises the diversity of ways of celebrating within the Muslim community, and teachers can illustrate this using the different examples given. This will also provide opportunity to compare with similar and different practices of other religions.

✦ Where time permits, the inclusion of a craft-type activity helps make learning more fun, and creates involvement and participation.

✦ The folktales are there to provide an alternative way of exploring some of the values underlying the faith. Stories offer an indirect way to explore spiritual values, through discussion, re-enactment, writing, and other creative activities.

Obviously this material does not need to be used only to explore a particular festival. It contains adequate material to provide a complete overview of Islam, as all the basic elements of Islamic belief are covered in the text.

In England an eight-level framework is used to cover stages in religious education. Below are examples of how the book might be used at each stage.

Level	Expectations	Possible activities arising from this book
1	Pupils know outlines of religious stories, recognise symbols and words and identify their own reactions to these stories.	Tell the story of the Prophet in outline; retell in groups; explore questions and concerns.
2	Pupils know religious characteristics may be common to more than one faith; respond sensitively to beliefs of others.	Tell the Prophet's life and the five pillars of Islam. Explore communalities with the Old Testament and New (prophets, belief in one true God). Organise discussion to help validate diversity of belief in the group. See 'Juha's truth' below.
3	Pupils can make the link between religious beliefs and the practices of a religion. They begin to make links between the values of religion and their own attitudes and behaviour.	Sections 1 and 2 of each chapter may be taught together, so that the particular rituals of the religion are connected to the Prophet's life. Folktales may be used to explore particular values and pupils' response to those values.
4	Students begin to make detailed comparisons between the beliefs and forms of different religions; begin to develop ideas about key moral teachings within religion, and their own response.	Detailed comparisons may be made between the life of the Prophet and that of other religious leaders, between the five pillars and, for example, the five Buddhist precepts or the ten commandments, or between the method and content of prayer in Islam and in other religions. Stories in Chapters 6 and 7 offer opportunities for exploring morality and pupils' responses.
5	Pupils understand the main common elements in world religions, and what difference these make to the lives of individuals.	Explore ideas about obedience (Chapter 2), faith (Chapter 3), prayer (Chapter 4) and generosity (Chapter 6) in Islam and other faiths.

Level	Expectations	Possible activities arising from this book
6	Pupils understand key differences between particular religions. They understand religious and other perspectives on contemporary issues.	Compare the Prophet's life with others (Jesus, Moses) to find differences. Compare the five pillars of Islam with other religions to identify differences.
7	Explore the historical and cultural context of religion, and its effects in the world.	Beyond the scope of this book.
8	Explain the various influences on religious belief. Elaborate detailed ways that religious views can deal with modern moral issues.	Beyond the scope of this book.

The following story might be used when introducing the idea that different people believe different things, and that 'truth' is not always simple and straightforward.

Juha Speaks the Truth

One day Juha told the king that truth was the highest good, and that all should seek it with vigilance and determination. The king was persuaded, and was determined to do something about it. He issued a declaration that all his people must tell the truth from now on. Anyone caught lying would be hanged. He told his guards at the gates of the city that they should question everyone entering the gates. Those that told the truth should be allowed to pass, those that lied should be taken and hanged.

The next day Juha was entering the city when a guard stopped him.

'Where are you going?' asked the guard.

'To be hanged!' replied Juha grimly.

' Is that the truth?' asked the guard.

'You tell me,' replied Juha.

Well, the guard tried to puzzle it out.

'If I take him and hang him then he will have told the truth so I can't hang him, but if I don't hang him then he will have told a lie so I will have to hang him! What shall I do?'

The guard couldn't decide so he took Juha to see the king. The king looked displeased.

'What are you up to?' he asked.

'I wanted to show you,' replied Juha, 'That there are two types of truth here – your truth and mine!'

The king laughed and cancelled his decree.

Of course, the stories and ideas in this book need not be restricted to religious education, but can be included in literacy and creative writing work, citizenship education and many other areas.

211

213

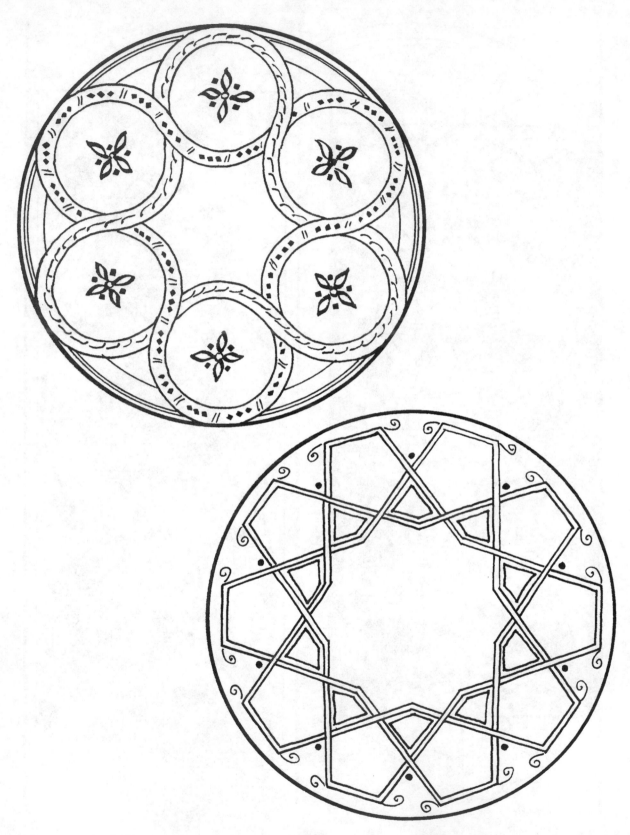

214

Other books from Hawthorn Press

Festivals Together
Guide to multicultural celebration
Sue Fitzjohn, Minda Weston, Judy Large

This special book for families and teachers helps you celebrate festivals from cultures from all over the world. This resource guide for celebration introduces a selection of 26 Buddhist, Christian, Hindu, Jewish, Muslim and Sikh festivals. It offers a lively introduction to the wealth of different ways of life. There are stories, things to make, recipes, songs, customs and activities for each festival, comprehensively illustrated.

224pp; 250 x 200mm; paperback; 1 869 890 46 9

Festivals, Family and Food
Guide to seasonal celebration
Diana Carey and Judy Large

This family favourite is a unique, well loved source of stories, recipes, things to make, activities, poems, songs and festivals. Each festival such as Christmas, Candlemas and Martinmas has its own, well illustrated chapter. There are also sections on Birthdays, Rainy Days, Convalescence and a birthday Calendar. The perfect present for a family, it explores the numerous festivals that children love celebrating.

224pp; 250 x 200mm; paperback; 0 950 706 23 X

The Children's Year
Seasonal crafts and clothes
Stephanie Cooper, Christine Fynes-Clinton, Marije Rowling

You needn't be an experienced craftsperson to create beautiful things! This step by step, well illustrated book with clear instructions shows you how to get started. Children and parents are encouraged to try all sorts of handwork, with different projects relating to the seasons of the year.

Here are soft toys, wooden toys, moving toys such as balancing birds or climbing gnomes, horses, woolly hats, mobiles and dolls. Over 100 treasures to make, in seasonal groupings.

192pp; 250 x 200mm; paperback;
1 869 890 00 0

All Year Round

Christian calendar of celebrations
Ann Druitt, Christine Fynes-Clinton, Marije Rowling

All Year Round is brimming with things to make; activities, stories, poems and songs to share with your family. It is full of well illustrated ideas for fun and celebration: from Candlemas to Christmas and Midsummer's day to the Winter solstice.

Observing the round of festivals is an enjoyable way to bring rhythm into children's lives and provide a series of meaningful landmarks to look forward to. Each festival has a special character of its own: participation can deepen our understanding and love of nature and bring a gift to the whole family.

320pp; 250 x 200mm; paperback; 1 869 890 47 7

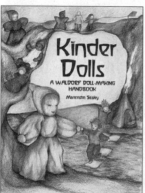

Kinder Dolls

A Waldorf doll-making handbook
Maricristin Sealey

Children treasure handmade dolls. Making a simple doll for a child is a gift for life, that encourages the magic of creative play. Kinder Dolls shows how to create hand-crafted dolls from natural materials. A range of simple, colourful designs will inspire both beginners and experienced doll makers alike. These dolls are old favourites, originating in Waldorf Steiner kindergartens where parents make dolls together for their children, and for the school.

160pp; 246 x 189mm; paperback; 1 903458 03 X

Games Children Play

How games and sport help children develop
Kim Brooking-Payne
Illustrated by Marije Rowling

Games Children Play offers an accessible guide to games with children of age 3 upwards. These games are all tried and tested, and are the basis for the author's extensive teacher training work. The book explores children's personal development and how this is expressed in movement, play, songs and games.

Each game is clearly and simply described, with diagrams or drawings, and accompanied by an explanation of why this game is helpful at a particular age. The equipment that may be needed is basic, cheap and easily available.

192pp; 297 x 210mm; paperback; 1 869 890 78 7

Storytelling with Children
Nancy Mellon

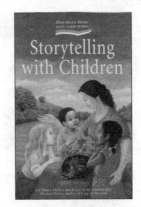

Telling stories awakens wonder and creates special occasions with children, whether it is bedtime, around the fire or on rainy days. Nancy Mellon shows how you can become a confident storyteller and enrich your family with the power of story.

'Nancy Mellon continues to be an inspiration for storytellers old and new. Her experience, advice and suggestions work wonders. They are potent seeds that give you the creative confidence to find your own style of storytelling.'
Ashley Ramsden, Director of the School of Storytelling, Emerson College

192pp; 216 x 138mm
paperback
1 903458 08 0

Celebrating Christmas Together
Nativity and Three Kings Plays with Stories and Songs
Estelle Bryer and Janni Nicol

Create the wonder of Christmas with your children at school or at home – starting with a simple Advent Calendar and Crib Scene. This Treasury includes the Nativity Play, with staging directions and instructions for simple costumes and props, plus songs and music to accompany the play.

96pp; 210 x 148mm
paperback; 1 903458 20 X

'A practical and beautiful guide to making Christmas a magical time for children.'
Sally Jenkinson, author of *The Genius of Play*

Christmas Stories Together
Estelle Bryer and Janni Nicol

Here is a treasure trove of 36 tales for children aged 3-9. The stories range from Advent through Christmas ending with the Holy Family's flight into Egypt – in fact, tales for the whole year. These stories will soon become family favourites, with their imaginative yet down to earth language and lively illustrations.

128pp; 210 x 148mm
paperback; 1 903458 22 6

'This book is alight with the genius of storytelling. It tenderly shows how to weave a pattern of stories over Advent and the twelve days of Christmas.'
Nancy Mellon, author of *Storytelling with Children*

Pull the Other One!
String Games and Stories Book 1
Michael Taylor

This well-travelled and entertaining series of tales is accompanied by clear instructions and explanatory diagrams – guaranteed not to tie you in knots and will teach you tricks with which to dazzle your friends!

128pp; 216 x 148mm; drawings; paperback; 1 869 890 49 3

'A practical and entertaining guide, which pulls together a wealth of ideas from different cultures and revives a forgotten art. I think parents as well as children will enjoy this book.'   Sheila Munro, parenting author

Now You See It...
String Games and Stories Book 2
Michael Taylor

String Games are fun, inviting children to exercise skill, imagination and teamwork. They give hands and fingers something clever and artistic to do! Following the success of *Pull the Other One!*, here are more of Michael Taylor's favourite string games, ideal for family travel, for creative play and for party tricks.

136pp; 216 x 148mm; paperback; 1 903458 21 8

For further information or a book catalogue, please contact:

Hawthorn Press,
1 Lansdown Lane, Stroud, Gloucestershire GL5 1BJ
Tel: (01453) 757040 Fax: (01453) 751138 E-mail: info@hawthornpress.com
Website: www.hawthornpress.com

If you have difficulties ordering Hawthorn Press books from a bookshop, you can order direct from:

Booksource, 32 Finlas Street, Glasgow G22 5DU
Tel: (08702) 402182 Fax: (0141) 557 0189 E-mail: orders@booksource.net

or you can order online at **www.hawthornpress.com**

Dear Reader

If you wish to follow up your reading of this book, please tick the boxes below as appropriate, fill in your name and address and return to Hawthorn Press:

☐ Please send me a catalogue of other Hawthorn Press books.

☐ Please send me details of Festivals events and courses.

Questions I have about *Festivals* are:

Name _____

Address _____

_____

Postcode _____ Tel. no. _____

Please return to:

Hawthorn Press, 1 Lansdown Lane, Stroud, Gloucestershire. GL5 1BJ, UK
or Fax (01453) 751138